Foreword

Dr. Vikas Chaturvedi

Chairman, ASSOCHAM Europe (Netherlands)
Chairman, Institute of Chartered Accountants of India, Netherlands Chapter
Chairman, Valuecent Group

The Netherlands has created a niche place for itself in this Global Trade and investment scenario with its strategic coastal location and access to 500 million consumers in western Europe. With an excellent logistics infrastructure, excellent IT connectivity, internationally-oriented workforce and favorable business and tax climate, The Netherlands is a Natural Gateway to Europe.

India on the other side is in a very interesting phase of its development. India is expected to become USD 5 trillion economy by 2025 and offers significant opportunities.

The bilateral ties between India and Netherlands can be productive to both the economies since The Netherlands remains among the top 10 partners of India in terms of trade volume. Netherlands is the 6th largest investor in India and likewise India is the 5th largest investor in The Netherlands.

As we move forward, the ties are only going to be strengthened between the two Natural Partners and will see some exciting developments and benefits for both. ASSOCHAM Netherlands is delighted to release this book in collaboration with NFIA and look forward to support Indian companies who are looking to invest in Europe.

I am very grateful to NFIA who agreed to support this book, team of ASSOCHAM Netherlands (in particular Prachee, Sandra and Sushmita) and all the people who have directly or indirectly contributed to the publication of book.

May 2018!

Ms. Stans Kleijnen

Executive Director, Netherlands Foreign Investment Agency, India

I am delighted to present the "Holland: Investment and Trade Opportunities" study that we have prepared in collaboration with ASSOCHAM, Europe. Through this study, we are providing our perspectives on why India and Europe are natural partners, why the Netherlands truly is India's gateway to Europe and how our Dutch Government agencies can help Indian companies in their European ambitions.

As many Indian companies have already discovered, The Netherlands is an excellent gateway to the European market. Schiphol airport and Rotterdam's seaport provide easy access to the European continent. So, it should come as no surprise that trade between our two nations is at an all-time high. And about 200 Indian companies have already set up shop in the Netherlands.

In this study, we present fourteen successful Indian companies and organizations that are active in different sectors in the Netherlands. These companies explain why they choose the Netherlands for their international expansion, what they do in the Netherlands and highlight which factors contribute to their success. Apart from that, the book also provides useful advice on doing business in the Netherlands as well as an overview of the business support tools provided by the Netherlands Foreign Investment Agency. I am sure you will find the interviews with both the Dutch and Indian Ambassadors, our regional colleagues and myself useful.

When Indian companies have ambitions to take their business to Europe, they can count on the Netherlands Foreign Investment Agency to help them on their way and assure a soft landing. With our offices in New Delhi, Mumbai and Bangalore, Netherlands Foreign Investment Agency looks forward to assisting you in your quest to the European market!

May 2018!

Executive Summary

India has developed into a rapidly expanding economy, focused on technological development and technical and scientific cooperation. Economic and commercial ties between India and Netherlands are an important facet of overall Indo-Dutch relations. Indo-Dutch bilateral relations have continued to develop and gain momentum in the past years. The main plank of the bilateral ties has been the strong economic and commercial relations. Both the Indian and the Dutch governments attach great importance to the bilateral economic relationship. The highlight of 2017, which was the 70th anniversary of the diplomatic relationship between India and the Netherlands, was the visit of PM Modi to the Netherlands in June 2017. The visit provided a significant boost to the bilateral ties, which have become multifaceted and encompass co-operation in various areas. In terms of trade and investment, India has strong economic interests in the Netherlands, as Netherlands is at present the sixth largest investor of FDI into India and is the 28th largest trading partner globally and 6th largest trading partner in the EU.

The Netherlands is steadily becoming an attractive destination for investments from India and figures amongst the top destinations. There are over 200 Indian companies having a presence in the Netherlands. These include all the major IT companies such as TCS, HCL, Wipro, Infosys, Tech Mahindra, NIIT, etc. Other prominent companies include Moser Baer, ONGC Videsh, Sun Pharma, Tata Steel, Kirloskar Brothers, Dr. Reddy's Labs, Jet Airways, Serum Institute, etc.

In light of convergence of economic and political interests, both countries see value in enhanced dialogue and have constantly striven to strengthen bilateral relations and expanding the framework of co-operation in various areas like agriculture, food processing, infrastructure, healthcare, science & technology and cybersecurity. This book gives a detailed overview on doing business in the Netherlands and will act as a useful tool for any investor looking to invest into the Netherlands and/or European market through the Netherlands.

Happy reading !!

May 2018

Contents

I. India - Netherlands: Links in historical perspective

The first ship of the Netherlands East India Company reached the famous Malabar Coast in Kerala, known as a Spice Coast about 1615, i.e. around 400 years ago. Off the beaten track, one can find remains of the Dutch period along the entire coastline from Surat to Kolkata and from Visakhapatnam to Kochi and Pullicat. Successive Dutch envoys to India proudly recall that when India attained Independence on 15th August 1947, the Dutch Ambassador was only one of the three Ambassadors present in Delhi at Prime Minister Nehru's famous "Tryst with Destiny" speech.

Our strategic position, each on our own continent, thus creates opportunities to work with each other. Our countries were at the starting and end-points of the *'Spice Route'*. India-Netherlands relations have acquired *a 'new momentum'* today. The Netherlands has identified India as a *'priority country'* for economic engagement. India and the Netherlands are uniquely placed to be *'preferred partners'* in key sectors. The objective is to take the Indo-Dutch relations to the *'next level'*. Political commitment on both sides is clear and manifest. India-EU strategic partnership was launched in 2004 during the Dutch Presidency of EU. The summit between the Dutch and Indian Prime Ministers in New Delhi on June 5, 2015, and the roadmap for cooperation charted by the two has given a fresh impetus to the bilateral relationship. Prime Minister Modi's visit to the

Netherlands in June 2017 further strengthened these ties. In fact, the bilateral relations today are perhaps the best they have ever been.

The Netherlands has the largest community of Indian Diaspora in Continental Europe, outside UK. In the last 15 years, the Indian community in the Netherlands has exponentially grown as more Indian companies continue to set up European headquarters – especially in Amstelveen where the numbers of Indian expats are the largest minority community having overtaken the Japanese. Furthermore numbering 220,000, the Indian diaspora includes the Hindustani community those who came to the Netherlands from India via Suriname. A community that is proud of their Indian heritage and culture which translates into strong support of India.

II. India and the Netherlands: A broad macro perspective

Built on the delta of some of Europe's main rivers, the Netherlands is a small country that punches above its weight in world business and politics. The Netherlands is geographically small with a size of 41,543Sq Km (smaller than the state of Haryana in India with a size 44,212 sq Km), densely populated (17 million people) with a highly strategic commercial location, with Europe's largest port (by volume) in Rotterdam. In terms of population, the Netherlands is the largest of the small countries of Western Europe. It is significantly smaller than neighbouring countries such as France, the United Kingdom and Germany, but also considerably more populated than countries of a similar size, such as Belgium, Denmark and Switzerland. The Netherlands is one of the most densely populated countries in the world. It has a growing and healthy economy with a strong services sector and excellent industries such as life sciences, electronics, agri-food, the chemical industry, water technology, and engineering. Additionally, it offers local and foreign businesses an environment that is conducive to international trade, efficient export, innovation and collaboration with some of the world's best companies and research institutes. The Netherlands economy is the **16th** largest in the world and the **fifth** largest in the European Union, despite a population of just 16.9 million.

The Indo-Dutch relationship is shaped by government-to-government relations, but also by our business communities. **Now, the Netherlands is 6th largest investor in India and India is a significantly 5th largest investor in the Netherlands.** India received U.S. $ 3.2 billion in investment from the Netherlands in 2016-17 (RBI, Annual Report,2016-17). Bilateral trade between India and Holland amounts to **around 7 billion** Dollars and continues to grow. India and the Netherlands are working together in many areas, including agriculture, water management, logistics, urban planning, life sciences, healthcare, sports and CSR. Various Dutch multinationals and SME's are based in India, and many have set up their R&D centers there too. There is, however, scope for more.

Dutch companies lead the global pack in key areas such as chemicals, electronics, maritime engineering, energy, infrastructure and creative industries. No wonder some of the world's leading multinationals are homegrown & headquartered in the Netherlands, among them: Royal Dutch Shell, Unilever, Philips and Heineken. International trade routes converge at Rotterdam, the largest port in Europe, and at Amsterdam Airport Schiphol, a major international air logistics hub. **Amsterdam is a major global financial Centre, a position the city has held since the Dutch East India Company (VOC) invented shares in 1602,** and the first stock exchange was set up here.

III. The Netherlands: The Gateway to Europe

The Netherlands: A central location

The Netherlands has a strategic coastal location with access to some 500 million consumers in Western Europe. Also, it is located in the center of the three biggest economies in Europe: Germany, the United Kingdom and France and known for an international outlook and openness to foreign investment. It has excellent logistics infrastructure including the Port of Rotterdam which is the largest in Europe and a renowned international hub Amsterdam Airport Schiphol. Not to mention its excellent ICT connectivity, internationally-oriented workforce (who speak excellent English) and favourable business and tax climate. The Netherlands is also a wonderful place to live, with a good standard of living, safe cities and top-notch schools. It is home to more than 6,000 foreign companies with more than 8,000 operations. What's more, 160 million consumers can be reached within 24 hours of Amsterdam or Rotterdam, making the Netherlands the perfect springboard into the European market. Its proximity to clients and consumers is unparalleled, for instance, 170 million consumers are within a distance of 300 miles (500 Kms) and 244 million consumers within a distance of 600 miles (1000 Kms).

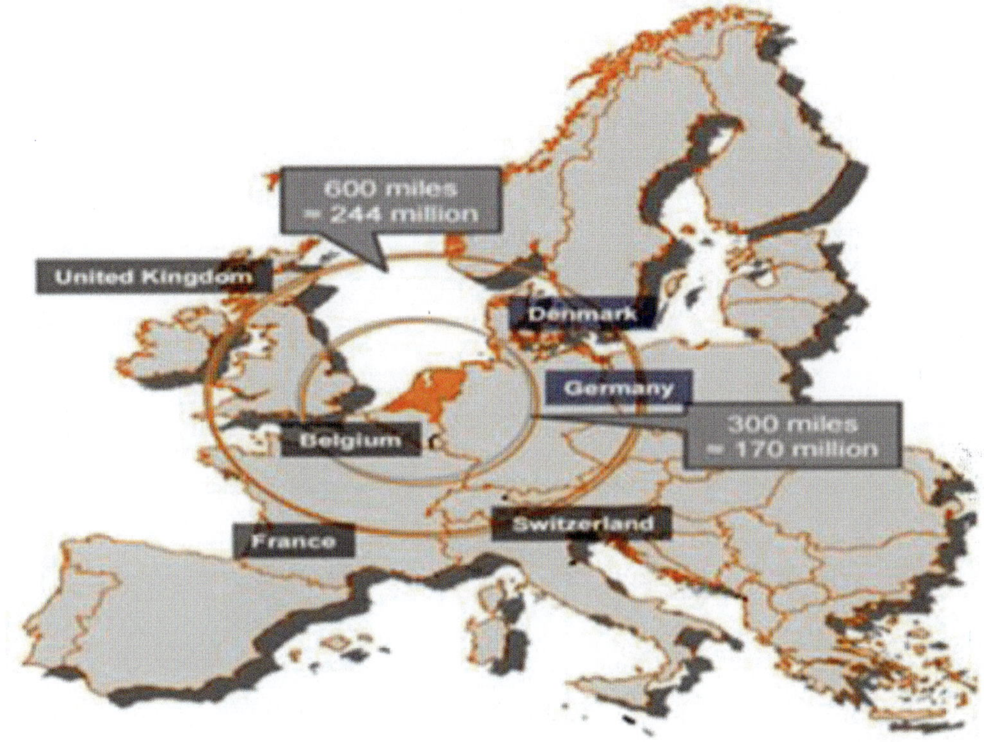

Overview of population in ambit of The Netherlands

Seamless accessibility to Europe

The Netherlands is an outstanding location: a natural gateway with flat countryside and good river connections has been built into a dense infrastructure of well-maintained roads, railways, inland waterways, airports and seaports. It has (i) Four international airports (including Amsterdam Airport Schiphol and Rotterdam-The Hague Airport) ;(ii) Main ports Rotterdam (387 million tons of transshipments) and Amsterdam (87 million tons) ;(iii) 85,000 miles of public roads, of which 3,200 miles highways; (iv) 1,750 miles of railway;(v) 3,235 miles of waterways for inland shipping; and (vi) about 11,185 miles of pipelines (for gas, oil and refined products).

Top class accessibility

Stable and vibrant parliamentary democracy

The Netherlands is a stable and vibrant parliamentary democracy, recognized worldwide for its transparency, fairness and effectiveness. The legal system is fair and transparent and well equipped to deal with business, trade, taxation and patent issues. There are specialized courts for dealing with criminal and administrative issues, as well as with tax law, planning law, environmental law and trade and commerce. There is a rich variety of world-class law firms –both home grown and large international ones – that can provide assistance with tax law, mergers and acquisitions, and European law. The Hague is the seat of the European Patent Office. Besides, **the Netherlands is host to important global international legal organizations**: The Permanent Court of Arbitration, the International Court of Justice, The Hague Conference on Private International Law, the

EU's criminal intelligence agency, Europol, and the EU's judicial cooperation agency, Eurojust. It is also host to the Organization for the Prohibition of Chemical Weapons (OPCW).

Dutch cities: some highlights

Amsterdam
- 4th best major European city of the future. (2016/2017)
- Key industries: creative industries, ICT, life sciences and health, R&D, logistics and tourism sector.

Utrecht
- Key industries: IT (software), life science and gaming.
- 2nd best mid-sized European city for connectivity and 3rd on human capital and lifestyle.

The Hague
- Seat of the national government
- International city of Peace and Justice.

Rotterdam
- Hosts the largest and most important port in Europe.
- Europe's leading city in connectivity. (2016/2017)
- Key industries: energy, industry, logistic hub, medical sector, maritime, chemical creative sector & financial and service industry.

Eindhoven
- 4th best small European city of the future. (2016/2017)
- 'Eindhoven is hands-down most inventive city in the world' Forbes Magazine (2013).
- Key industries in the province: R&D and manufacturing in IT, high tech and food.

Well-developed financial system

The Netherlands has a well-developed financial system that is largely focused on global financial markets and trends. It is centered largely in Amsterdam, which hosts some of the most notable global banks of Dutch origin, among them ING Group, Rabobank and ABN AMRO, and large international banks. In addition, Netherlands is host to a broad range of private equity investors and venture capital funds, as well as trust fund managers. Amsterdam, the country's financial center, hosts the Euronext Amsterdam exchange, which is part of NYSE Euronext, as well as Atradius, the world's largest credit risk management company. ABP is one of the largest pension funds in the world.

Home to innovative solutions to global challenges

The world turns to the Netherlands for innovative solutions to global challenges such as food supply and security, water supply, flood control, climate change, renewable energy, waste management and infrastructure. Countries around the world call in Dutch expertise to dredge harbours; build dikes and bridges; develop new land; set up sustainable farms; implement water supply systems; improve infrastructure, and create renewable sources of energy. Many cutting-edge innovations and inventions used around the world also stem from Dutch research and laboratories. Dutch knowledge institutes collaborate with business and government within industry clusters, pooling knowledge and resources to create modern technologies and techniques. For instance, Brainport Eindhoven, also known as the Silicon Valley of Europe, is a hub where high tech giants such as Philips and ASML collaborate with researchers and start-up companies to develop new concepts and technologies.

The European Single Market Policy

As the fifth-largest exporter of goods in the world, the Netherlands occupies a prominent position when it comes to world trade. In 2016, the Netherlands exported goods worth a total of almost US$ 570 billion, which is about 3.6% of the world's total exports. The Netherlands is also a significant exporter of commercial services: exports of commercial services amounted to US$ 177 billion in 2016.

The role of the Netherlands as a key distribution location is also indicated by the volume of import and export activities. Almost 72 % of Dutch exports remain within the EU, especially Western Europe. Germany is easily the Netherlands' most significant trading partner, followed by Belgium, the United Kingdom and France. In addition, United States, China, Switzerland, Turkey and rest of the countries accounted for 4.2 %, 2%, 1.3%, 1.3 % and 19.3% of Dutch exports to the world respectively.

The Netherlands is the world's second largest exporter of food and agriculture (estimated at $78.3 billion in 2015) and the world's largest flower and bulb exporter (U.S. $ 3.9 billion in 2015) But the Netherlands is much more than an agrarian economy. Dutch agriculture is highly intensive and export focused. The temperate climate, fertile soils, and educated labor force make the Netherlands a highly productive agricultural producer; however, the large and sophisticated food processing industry accounts for a significant portion of exports. Without a doubt, the motor behind Holland's exports are its agri-food and horticulture sectors.

In terms of product decomposition, goods exports from the Netherlands mainly consist of machinery and equipment (about 31 percent of total exports in 2015), chemical products (about 17 percent), food products (about 13 percent) and natural gas and refinery products (about 18 percent). Re-exports—largely handled by multinational enterprises represent about 45 percent of total exports. They explain about a quarter of the trade surplus, pointing to the significant position of the Rotterdam port as a major transit location for European trade flows. Importantly, re-exports appear to increasingly account for the bulk of high value-added goods such as pharmaceutical products or office machinery. In terms of geographical breakdown, the largest share of the Dutch trade surplus is achieved with European partners, including Germany, while the country records a large and increasing deficit with the rest of the world, notably China. Throughout the period, the services balance has been small and negative, in contrast to the substantial inward and outward flows of intellectual property and business services traded by multinational enterprises (IMF, March 2017).

Imports into the Netherlands

As well as being a major exporter, the Netherlands also imports large quantities of goods: US$ 503 billion in 2016. With about 3.1% share of the global total, the country is the eight-largest importer of goods in the world. The Netherlands is also a significant importer of commercial services - imports of commercial services amounted to US$ 169 billion in 2016.

In 2015, 53 % of all imports into the Netherlands originated in the EU followed by China 9 %, U.S.A. 8.5 %, Russian Federation 3.6 %, Norway 3.1 % and others 22.8 %. Within the EU, Germany and Belgium were the main source of imports. Almost half of all products purchased by the Netherlands in Germany were related to chemical products and machinery. Of all the cars imported into the Netherlands, more than 90% came from Europe, particularly Belgium, France and Germany.

Cradle of creativity

Famed Dutch creativity could be seen and tapped in areas like water management, agri-food and infrastructure; these are areas in which the Netherlands enjoys a worldwide reputation. But some of Holland's most popular export products today come from the creative industries: television formats, music, fashion, architecture and serious and casual gaming. Dutch-made television shows such as The Voice, Big Brother and Splash, are being adopted by broadcast companies around the world. Some of the world's most popular games come from the Netherlands, including Killzone by Guerilla. Dutch DJ Armin van Buuren, DJ Tiestoaswell as well as DJ Hardwell all have been voted world's best DJ in the last decade. Meanwhile, Dutch designers such as MarliesDekkers and Viktor and Rolf are redefining fashion while super models such as DoutzenKroes and Lara Stone are giving a Dutch face to international fashion.

Dutch Trade Policy

The European Union (EU) is now a trading bloc comprising 28 countries in Europe. All Member States adopt common external trade policy and measures. Meanwhile, 19 EU Members, including Austria, Belgium, Cyprus, Estonia, Finland, France, Germany, Greece, Ireland, Italy, Latvia, Lithuania, Luxembourg, Malta, the Netherlands, Portugal, Slovakia, Slovenia and Spain, have adopted the euro as their legal tender. The United Kingdom is the only full Member State which has decided to exit the EU. It held a referendum on June 23, 2016 to decide whether it should remain a member of the European Union. Referendum resulted in a vote in favour of leaving the EU.

The EU's Common Commercial Policy covers all the main measures affecting trade in goods and services and almost all trade-related issues. Trade-related areas partially covered by the common trade policy include: company law, indirect taxation, standards and other technical regulations, and enforcement of intellectual property rights.

One of the most important aspects of the EU trade policy is that the EU is a customs union. The same import duties are charged on imports from third countries regardless of the country of entry into the EU. The main principles of customs law are regulated at EU level, although the customs authorities of the EU Member States oversee their application. **All Members of the EU have adopted a common trade policy towards imports from third countries.** The EU has a relatively liberal import regime. In general, import licensing is not required for products entering an EU country, except for certain sensitive products like agricultural goods, tobacco, weapons, etc., and products governed by quantitative restrictions (i.e. quotas) and surveillance. The EU has also restrictions and prohibitions regarding the importation of pirated or counterfeit goods and some chemical products containing hazardous substances, restrictions on genetically modified organisms and imports of live animals and animal products. The EU also applies trade defense measures against imports from third countries under various EU trade defense instruments, the main ones being anti-dumping (AD), countervailing (CV) and safeguard instruments. As at 31 January 2017, the EU had in place 53 AD measures and five CV against Chinese mainland-origin products.

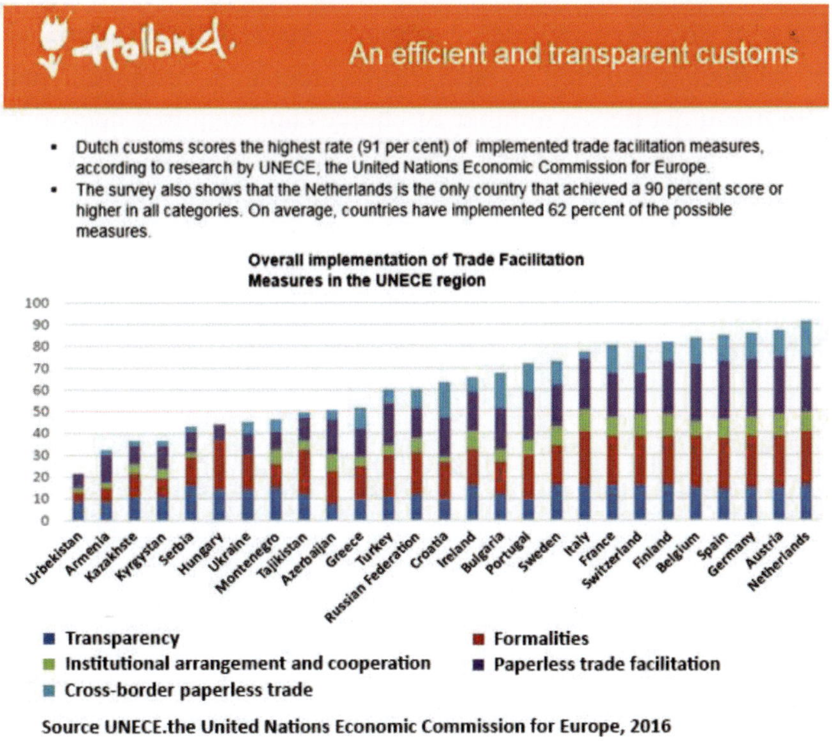

Standards

The Netherlands uses 2,000 specifically Dutch standards, 6,000 EU standards and 9,000 international standards. As a member of the EU, the Netherlands applies the product standards and certification approval processes developed by the EU. The Treaty of Rome requires all EU members to incorporate approved EU directives into its national laws.

As part of the programmed to establish common standards for all member countries, the EU regulates key product areas to protect the health and safety of consumers, as well as the environment. Many products require CE marking before they can be sold in the European Economic Area (EU + Iceland, Lichtenstein and Norway). CE marking proves that the product has been assessed and meets EU safety, health and environmental protection requirements. It is valid for products manufactured both inside and outside the EEA, that are then marketed inside the EEA. CE marking is valid only for products for which EU specifications have been introduced. The CE mark relates only to the mandatory health, safety, and environmental requirements established by the EU; it does not indicate conformity to European product standards. National marks of conformity with product standards remain compatible with the CE mark and both may be applied to the product. The CE mark replaces all national safety marks for the regulated products. To sell products in the Netherlands, exporters are required to apply CE marking whenever their product is covered by specific product legislation. CE marking product legislation offers manufacturers a number of choices and requires decisions to determine which safety/health concerns need to be addressed, which conformity assessment module is best suited to the manufacturing process, and whether or not to use EU-wide harmonized standards.

World Talent Ranking 2017

Common external tariff

A common external tariff is applicable to other countries, including India. The Netherlands applies EU tariffs, which are based on the international Harmonized System of product classification. Duty rates on manufactured goods from India generally range from five to eight percent and are usually based on the C.I.F. value of the goods at the port of entry. The C.I.F. value is the price of the goods (usually the sales price) plus packing costs, insurance, and freight charges to the port of entry. Most raw materials enter duty free or at low rates. Agricultural products face higher rates and special levies. Imports of food and agricultural commodities from outside the EU covered by the Common Agricultural Policy are subject to higher customs duty and quotas and may require a license or certificate.

Table:1- India & European Union (EU): Import Tariff Summary									
	Simple Average Bound			**Smpl Avg MFN Applied 2016**			**Trade Wt. Average, 2015**		
	Total	Agr	Non Agr	Total	Agr	Non Agr	Total	Agr	Non Agr
India	48.5 (74.4)	113.5	34.5 (70.5)	13.4	32.7	10.2	7.6	38.0	5.6
EU	5.0 (100.0)	11.9	3.9 (100.0)	5.2	11.1	4.2	3.0	7.8	2.6

Note: Smpl - Avg-simple average; Wt.-weighted Figures within parenthesis indicate percentage of bound tariff lines to total tariff lines. Agr - agriculture; Non Agr - non- agriculture

Source: World Tariff Profiles,2017https://www.wto.org/english/res_e/booksp_e/tariff_profiles17_e.pdf

Status of India and the EU Trade and Investment Agreement (BTIA)

In order to deepen and strengthen trade and investment relations between India and the EU, negotiations are currently underway for a Broad-based Trade and Investment Agreement (BTIA). In September 2005, the 6th India-EU Summit held in New Delhi decided to establish a High-Level Trade Group (HLTG) to explore ways and means to widen and broaden the economic relationship and explore possibility of a trade and investment agreement. In October 2006, the HLTG presented its report to the 7th India EU Summit at Helsinki. The summit decided that the two sides should enter into negotiations for the trade and investment agreement. The India-EU BTIA negotiations started in June 2007. Sixteen rounds of negotiations have been held so far, the last being held in March 2013 at Brussels. Recently, three stock taking meetings have taken place in India- EU BTIA on 18th January 2016 (in New Delhi), 22nd February 2016 (in Brussels) and on 15th July 2016 (in New Delhi). Recently, Commerce and Industry Minister Suresh Prabhu indicated resumption of negotiations of the long-stalled free trade pact between India and European Union.

A tax regime geared to attract foreign investment and foster entrepreneurship

A more friendly tax regime introduced in the late 1990s and a drop in the corporate tax rate to 25% in 2011 (announced further drop to 21% in 2021) make the Netherlands an attractive location for European operations. The Netherlands is known for its favourable fiscal climate and the high degree of customer service its tax authorities provide to foreign investors. Transparent, precise tax guidance lets investors know what to expect regarding long-term tax obligations. To this end, Advance Tax Rulings (ATR), in combination with Advance Pricing Agreements (APA), are guarantees given by local tax inspectors regarding long-term tax commitments for an acquisition or Greenfield operation.

Competitive Direct Tax System

Direct tax regime in Holland is geared to attract foreign investment and to foster entrepreneurship. In addition, the Netherlands offers a supportive fiscal climate for international companies, a wide tax treaty network, special measures for highly skilled expats and certainty in advance of future tax positions—just a few of the features that help multinational companies to thrive in the Netherlands.

- **Competitive statutory corporate income tax rate**

Corporate income tax is levied at the following rates (2018): (i) € 0 - € 200,000 subject to 20% and; (ii) 25% for taxable profits exceeding €200,000. Following the governmental coalition agreement, the corporate income tax is expected to be reduced in sections as from 2019. As per 2021, the rates are expected to drop to (i) 16% and (ii) 21%. A special optional tax rate may be elected for (patented) intangible assets. Under this option, the net income from intellectual property will be taxed at an effective tax rate of 7%.

- **Ruling Practice: certainty in advance**

The possibility of obtaining an Advance Tax Ruling (ATR) or an Advance Pricing Agreement (APA) is one of the most attractive features of Dutch tax law. The aim of the Dutch tax ruling policy is to attract international investors to the Netherlands by providing them certainty about their future tax position. The Dutch Tax Administration has a dedicated APA/ATR-team operating out of Rotterdam. The ATR regime has following distinct features: (a) An APA provides certainty in advance on the fiscal acceptability of the price (transfer pricing) that the Dutch group company pays to or receives from a foreign group company for receiving or delivering services or goods; (b)

An ATR is an agreement on the tax characterization of international corporate structures, such as certainty in advance on the application of the participation exemption.

- **Innovation Box: effective tax rate of 7%**

Companies can benefit from an effective tax rate of only 7% for profits derived from self-developed intangible assets for which a so-called WBSO declaration (for wage tax purposes) has been obtained. Intangible assets developed by another party for the risk and account of a Dutch taxpayer also qualify for the innovation box. The innovation box regime has the following relevant features:

- **R&D tax credit (WBSO): 32% / 14% wage tax reduction**

  a) The WBSO (R&D tax credit) of the Dutch Ministry of Economic Affairs is intended to provide entrepreneurs with an incentive to invest in research;

  b) With the WBSO, companies can lower the wage costs for R&D and other R&D costs and expenditures, such as prototypes or research equipment. The tax benefit can be set off in the tax return to the Dutch Tax and Customs Administration;

  c) For companies the R&D payroll tax deduction amounts to 32% of the first €350,000 of R&D wage and other costs and expenses, and 14% of all further R&D costs and expenses. For startups the tax deduction for the first €350,000 spent on R&D is even higher (40%);

  d) Self-employed entrepreneurs are entitled to a fixed R&D tax deduction of €12,623 and start-ups and self-employed entrepreneurs are entitled to an additional deduction of €6,315;

  e) There is no longer a maximum allowance per calendar year for each company (or corporate entity).

  f) The above-mentioned percentages and amounts are valid for 2018 only.

- **MIA/Vamil: tax relief schemes for environmentally friendly investments**

  a) The MIA scheme allows entrepreneurs to deduct up to 36% of the cost of an environmentally friendly investment from the fiscal profit, provided that the investment is listed on the Environment List. The investment amount must be at least € 2,500 per asset. The maximum investment amount for which a deduction is granted is € 25,000,000 in 2017. The Vamil scheme let's entrepreneurs decide for themselves when to write off 75% of their investment costs listed on the Environment List. That in turn offers an advantage in terms of liquidity and interest. For the other 25% of the investment costs entrepreneurs follow the regular investment rebate;

b) All Dutch entrepreneurs paying income or corporate tax are eligible to apply for the MIA/Vamil schemes;

c) The Environmental List shows all the investments eligible for the MIA scheme, the Vamil scheme or both;

d) The Environmental List contains hundreds of items of investment, or capital assets, which cause less environmental damage and are often in advance of the legal requirements. The list is updated annually.

- **Energy Investment Allowance (EIA): tax relief program for sustainable energy**

a) Companies that invest in energy-saving installations, or that make use of sustainable energy, may deduct a certain percentage of the invested sum from their taxable profits from the year in which the goods are purchased.;

b) 54.5% of the relevant expenditures is deductible from the taxable earnings in the year in which the equipment is purchased;

c) Each business can qualify for the EIA for energy investments of a minimum of € 2,500 and a maximum of € 121 million in a calendar year;

d) EIA is applicable under certain conditions, such as (i) The company must have an environmental permit or a building permit;(ii) The energy list states which types of equipment qualify for the program;(iii) The energy advice connected with the purchase can be included in the deduction, as well as additional costs needed to make an assetoperational;(iv) Any investment grant that was received for the relevant asset must be deducted from the acquisition or production costs (operating subsidies need not be deducted, however).

- **Participation Exemption: drive for European Headquarters**

The participation exemption, one of the most important provisions of Dutch corporate income tax legislation, explains the large number of European Headquarters in the Netherlands. The objective of the exemption is to avoid double taxation when the profits of a subsidiary are distributed to its parent company.

a) Under the participation exemption, dividends and capital gains/losses are fully exempt from corporate income tax (i.e. for capital gains, this means that gains are not taxed while capital losses are not deductible, except for qualifying liquidation losses).

b) The participation exemption may be applicable without additional requirements for shareholdings of 5% or more provided that the shareholding is not considered to be held as a portfolio investment;

c) A shareholding is generally not considered to be held as a portfolio investment if the shares are not held for a return that may be expected from normal asset management (motive test). This is e.g. based on the functions and assets of the shareholding. The test is based on long-standing Dutch case law and will provide for a flexible basis to obtain tax rulings regarding the application of the Dutch participation exemption;

d) If the non-portfolio investment condition is not met, the Dutch tax payer may still benefit from the participation exemption, if: (i) the passive shareholding itself is subject to a tax rate of 10% or more; or and; (ii) the assets of the subsidiary do not largely (more than 50%) consist of low taxed (less than 10%) portfolio investment

- **Fiscal Unity Regime: consolidated tax returns**

a) This provides for a tax consolidation of companies within a group by filing a consolidated tax return;

b) One of the main advantages is that losses of one company can be set off against profits of another;

c) Within the fiscal unity assets can be transferred from one company to another without levying corporate income tax.

d) Transactions between companies which are part of a fiscal unity are not subject to corporate income tax

- **Transfer Pricing: arm's length principles**

a) Dutch corporate tax law contains the provision that intra-company pricing for goods and services must be at arm's length;

b) Guidelines for intra-company pricing are given by extensive policy based upon the arm's length principles for intercompany pricing as contained in the OECD model tax treaty and the OECD transfer pricing guidelines.;

c) It is possible to obtain APA on transfer pricing issues.

- **Carrying Losses: up to nine years**

a) Loss carry-over facilities in the Netherlands are liberal;

b) Both resident and non-resident taxpayers have a loss carry-back possibility of one year and a carry forward possibility of nine years. As part of the governmental coalition agreement, the carry forward possibility is expected to be reduced to six years. The losses need to be confirmed by the tax inspector by means of a loss statement;

c) Limitations for loss carry-over can apply when there is a significant change in ultimate shareholders;

d) A significant change occurs when a company ceases its business activities or reduces its business by more than 70%.

- **Wide Tax Treaty Network: avoidance of double taxation**

The Netherlands has one of the most extensive tax treaty networks in the EU, having concluded treaties for the avoidance of double taxation on income and capital with nearly 100 countries. In case no treaty applies, the Netherlands often unilaterally provides for double tax relief. Taxpayers may also benefit from favorable rules provided by EU directives and EU law. Most double taxation agreements negotiated by the Netherlands relating to income and capital gains have followed the draft models published by the Organization for Economic Cooperation and Development (OECD).

- **Treaty-based tax rate reductions**

a) **The Netherlands does not levy any withholding tax on interest payments or royalty payments by a Netherlands-based establishment**. As part of the governmental coalition agreement, this may change with reference to such payments made to low tax jurisdictions. These changes may be implemented as from 2020. Additionally, tax treaties usually reduce or eliminate the foreign withholding tax on interest or royalties paid to a Netherlands-based establishment.

Furthermore, the implementation laws based on the EU Interest and Royalty Directive eliminate the withholding tax for qualifying EU royalties and interest.

b) The Dutch statutory dividend withholding tax rate is 15%. However, the tax rate is reduced when a dividend distribution is made to a tax treaty protected shareholder (generally reduced to 5% or even 0%). Dividends paid to qualifying EU parent companies are exempt from dividend tax due to the implementation laws based on the EU Parent/Subsidiary Directive. As part of the coalition agreement of Government, the dividend withholding tax may eventually partly be abolished. With regard to low tax jurisdictions, the dividend withholding tax is expected to still be applicable (as per 2020).

- **30% Ruling: special tax regime for expats**

a) The Netherlands has a special tax regime for expatriates, the so-called 30% ruling, which provides a substantial income tax exemption of up to 30%, for a period of up to 96 months. This is viewed as a reimbursement for the extra costs involved in living abroad;

b) According to this rule, the employer may grant the employee a tax-free allowance of up to a maximum of 30% of his or her remuneration. The remuneration includes incidental and flexible forms of income such as bonus payments and stock options. Termination and pension payments are excluded;

c) In order to qualify for the 30% ruling, the following conditions must be met: (I) The employer must make a reasonable case that the employee possesses specific expertise that is not available, or is scarce in the Dutch labor market, by meeting the specified minimum taxable income levels along with certain additional conditions which include that the employee must be recruited from abroad, must be a Dutch wage tax-withholding agent and cannot be living abroad within a 150 km radius of the Dutch border;

d) The exemption is available for a period of 8 years (96 months). After a period of five years, the tax authorities can request that the employer demonstrate that the employee still meets the conditions. As part of the governmental coalition agreement, the period for the 30% ruling may be reduced to 5 years (60 months).

- **VAT Deferment: cash-flow advantages**

  a) Based upon its special position as a distribution country in the EU, the Netherlands offers under certain conditions a so-called deferment system, which gives a complete deferment until the quarterly VAT return;

  b) This system leads to a situation in which the VAT due at import is not paid at that moment but is deferred until filing of the quarterly VAT return. On the VAT return, the VAT must be declared but it can be deducted on the same form, thus preventing cash-flow complications;

  c) To obtain the license required to use this deferment system, a company must be registered for VAT in the Netherlands as a domestic entrepreneur or as a foreign entrepreneur with a permanent establishment for VAT in the Netherlands and have regular imports to the Netherlands.

- **Dutch Tax Authorities: Access to the tax inspector**

The Dutch tax and customs administration understands the need of investors with emphasis on certainty and advance ruling about how tax law will be applied in a specific case. To cater to the requirements of foreign investors **Dutch authorities have created 'Central Point for Potential Foreign Investors'**. The tax inspector for the area where the business is located will be bound by the agreements made with The Central Point. The Central Point works together with the APA/ATR team. This team concludes advance pricing agreements on transfer pricing issues and advance tax rulings on other issues of an international nature. The Dutch Tax Administration has a cooperative attitude towards taxpayers and aims for an enhanced relationship based on trust, transparency and mutual understanding. For this purpose, the Netherlands introduced a voluntary 'Horizontal Monitoring'-program. The greatest advantage of Horizontal Monitoring is that certainty in advance on tax issues is given as early as possible. As a result, fewer checks afterwards are necessary and the administrative burden is reduced.

Box: 1 Snapshot of Dutch Tax System (2018)

- **Attractive features of the Dutch tax regime include**
  - Relatively low statutory corporate income tax rate of 25% (20% for first 200,000 Euro);
  - Possibility of obtaining advance tax rulings from the Dutch tax authorities giving certainty on future tax position;
  - Innovation box resulting in an effective corporate tax rate of 7% for qualifying profits;
  - R&D tax credit for qualifying R&D wage costs and other R&D expenses and investments (WBSO;
  - Tax relief schemes for environmentally friendly investments (MIA/Vamil);
  - Tax relief program for sustainable energy (EIA);
  - Favorable participation exemption regime;
  - Fiscal unity regime which provides for a tax consolidation of companies within a corporate group, which freely offsets profits and losses among group members;
  - Transfer pricing practice in accordance with OECD Transfer Pricing Guidelines and the possibility to obtain an Advance Pricing Agreement (APA);
  - The possibility to carry forward losses for nine years and to carry them backward for one year;
  - Wide tax treaty network to avoid double taxation and reducing withholding taxes on dividends, interests and royalties (for interest and royalties often to 0%);
  - No statutory withholding tax on outgoing interest and royalty payments;
  - Favorable tax treatment for expats (30% tax ruling);
  - VAT deferment upon import: no upfront payment of VAT;
  - Dutch Tax Authorities: access to the tax inspector;
  - Dutch Customs Authorities: practical and pro-active approach

Benefits arising out of the India-Netherlands tax treaty

Dutch tax law comprises of a wide range of facilities and incentives relating to investments into the country, but also for having a coordinating role in international groups. The Netherlands offers considerable advantages given that under Dutch law, it is easy to migrate the effective place of management to the Netherlands and thereby become a tax resident of the country. The India-Netherlands tax treaty further provides that capital gains derived by Dutch residents from the sale of shares in an Indian company will be taxable only in the Netherlands so long as (a) the shares are not sold to an Indian resident; and (b) the shares do not derive value principally from immovable property in India. Coupled with other favorable aspects such as low withholding tax on dividend and lack of a Limitation of Benefits (LOB) clause, Netherlands may offer considerable tax efficiencies to foreign taxpayers. Tax treaties India has with other European jurisdictions such as France and Spain provide India the right to tax capital gains on the sale of shares only if the holding in the Indian company is at least 10 percent.

- **Value-added tax (VAT)**

Value-added tax, most frequently called by its acronym VAT, is charged on the sale of goods and services within the country. Unlike the customs duty, which is the same for all EU member countries, the VAT is established by the tax authorities of each country and differs from country to country. At each stage of the manufacturing and distribution chain, the seller adds the appropriate amount of VAT (tax on the amount of value that the seller added to the product, plus the amount of VAT passed on to the seller by the supplier) to the sales price. Below is a summary of the Dutch VAT rates.

- Zero percent rates apply to exports.
- Six percent rate applies to necessities such as food, qualifying medicines, and transportation.
- Twenty-one percent is the general or standard rate and applies to most goods.

As part of the governmental coalition agreement, the six percent rate may increase to nine percent as of 2019. For imports into the Netherlands, the VAT is levied at the same rate as for domestic products or transactions. The base on which VAT is charged on imports is the C.I.F. value at the port of entry, plus any duty, excise taxes, levies, or other charges (excluding the VAT) collected by customs at the time of importation. This total represents the transaction value of the import when it clears customs. The importer is liable for payment of customs duties, VAT, and any other charges at the time of clearing the goods through customs. Exports from the Netherlands are exempt from VAT since they are not consumed in the country, but will be subject to any tax imposed in the country of destination.

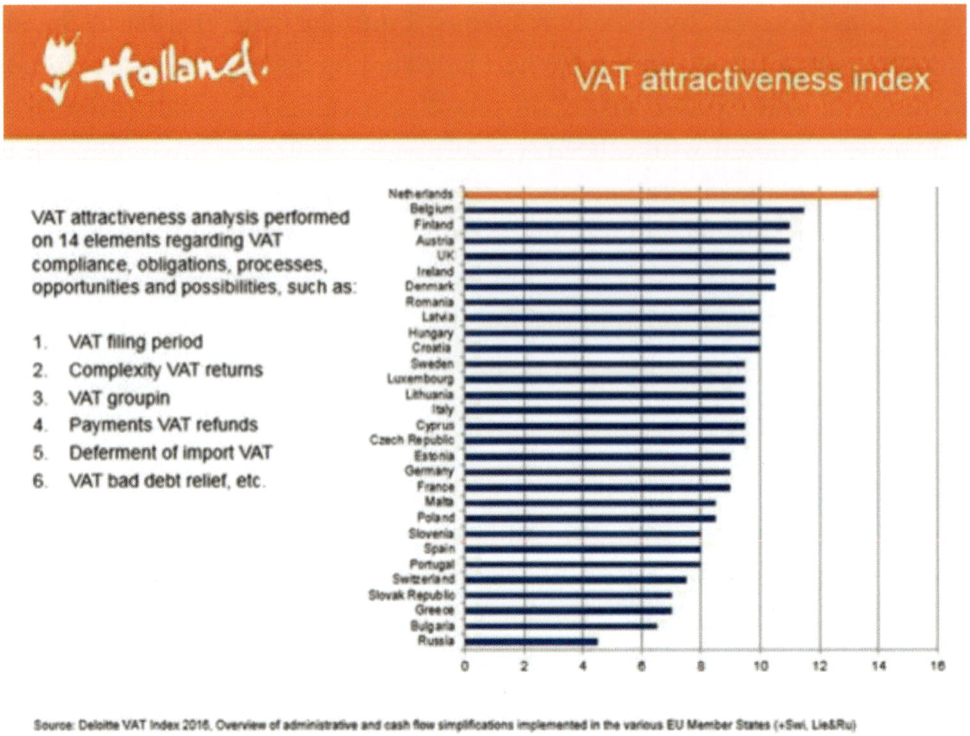

- **Dutch Customs Authorities: Practical and pro-active approach**

Goods that are brought into the European Union (EU) are, from the time of their entry, subject to Customs supervision, meeting the requirements laid down in the EU customs legislation. The Customs inspector understands the importance of a reliable government partner for enterprises. Where the import and export of goods are concerned, he is open to consultation in order to find the most suitable customs arrangements for your company. The Dutch Customs authorities are well known for their practical and pro-active approach towards facilitating international trade and optimizing customs procedures. This fact underlies the Netherlands' preferred status as a country in which to base importing activities. According to research carried out by UNECE (United Nations Economic Commission for Europe) in 2015, Dutch Customs achieve the highest score for overall implementation of trade facilitation measures in the UNECE region. This table shows the Netherlands achieved as core of 91 percent of implemented measures. The survey also showed that the Netherlands is the only country that reaches a level of implementation that is above 90% for each category of measures.

IV. Netherlands top destination for foreign direct investment (FDI)

In the UNCTAD 2017 World Investment Report, the Netherlands is ranked fifth in the global ranking of countries receiving the most FDI influx. The country is also the third global investor (in terms of investment outflows) behind the U.S. and China. Dutch investment policy is characterized by a strong international orientation and a liberal policy towards foreign investment. Many Dutch companies are multinational by nature and some of these are listed on foreign stock markets. Moreover, there are no regulatory restrictions on FDI into the Netherlands. The Netherlands is home to over 6000 companies with 100% foreign ownership. Over 20% of foreign owned companies established in the Netherlands are of U.S. origin. Although foreign-owned firms comprise just 2% of all firms located in the Netherlands, they account for 15% of private sector employment with 800.000 employees.

Table: 2 Netherlands as prime FDI Destination

Foreign Direct Investment	**2014**	**2015**	**2016**
FDI Inward Flow *(million USD)*	53,307	68,751	91,956
FDI inward Stock *(million USD)*	717,403	719,427	801,136
Number of Greenfield Investments***	209	241	199
FDI Inwards *(in % of GFCF****)*	33.6	47.1	60.1
FDI Stock *(in % of GDP)*	81.4	95.8	103.9

*Note: * The UNCTAD Inward FDI Performance Index is Based on a Ratio of the Country's Share in Global FDI Inflows and its Share in Global GDP. ** The UNCTAD Inward FDI Potential Index is Based on 12 Economic and Structural Variables Such as GDP, Foreign Trade, FDI, Infrastructures, Energy Use, R&D, Education, Country Risk.*

**** Green Field Investments Are a Form of Foreign Direct Investment Where a Parent Company Starts a New Venture in a Foreign Country by Constructing New Operational Facilities from the Ground Up. **** Gross Fixed Capital Formation (GFCF) Measures the Value of Additions to Fixed Assets Purchased by Business, Government and Households Less Disposals of Fixed Assets Sold Off or Scrapped.*

Source: Santander Trade Portal, Netherlands Foreign Investment

The Netherlands remained one of the world's top destinations for FDI stock at U.S. $ 801 billion in 2016, which accounted for a 3 per cent share of the global stock of FDI. The Netherlands received US$ 92 billion in FDI inflows in 2016. (**Table:2**). **The Netherlands is recipient of 5.3 % of world global FDI inflows and 9% of all FDI inflow into developed economies during 2016.** This reflects a **shift** over the last decade to the Netherlands as a key export platform and pan-regional distribution hub. The Netherlands regularly ranks as one of the most competitive industrialized countries on various international surveys, with an attractive business and investment climate. Among these, the World Economic Forum (WEF) Global Competitiveness Report 2017-18 places **the Netherlands in fourth** position among the world's most competitive economies and most competitive economy in the European Union. The top three are Switzerland, the United States and Singapore. Netherlands is in fourth place, followed by Germany, Hong Kong and Sweden. The Netherlands has maintained its position with the support of a strong education system and high levels of tech readiness among businesses and individuals. Its thriving innovation ecosystem, ranked 6th globally, puts the country in an excellent position to shape the unfolding Fourth Industrial Revolution.

FDI is concentrated in growth sectors including information and communication technology (ICT), biotechnology, medical technology, electronic components, and machinery and equipment. Investment projects are predominantly in value-added logistics, machinery and equipment, and (luxury) foods. The country's intellectual capital, commercial focus and collaborative approach make it an ideal partner for business and investment activities. Dutch researchers are driving or collaborating on cutting-edge research and their findings are regularly cited in many of the world's leading publications.

The Dutch comply with EU reciprocity provisions in banking and investment services, and apply non-discrimination, including in government incentives, national rules of incorporation, and access to the capital market. Commercial laws and regulations accord with international legal practices and standards, and apply equally to foreign and Dutch companies.

Air transport is governed by bilateral aviation treaty between the two countries and applicable EU regulation. Indian nationals can invest in Dutch/European carriers if the airline remains majority-owned by EU governments or nationals from EU member states. Additionally, the EU and its member states reserve the right to limit foreign investment in the voting equity of an EU airline on a reciprocal basis to that allowed by India for foreign nationals in Indian carriers.

More than 50% of Forbes 2,000 companies active in ICT maintain an office in the Amsterdam region. The Netherlands is the second most densely-cabled country in the world. The Amsterdam Internet hub, AMS-IX, is the largest data transport hub in the world. According to Eurostat, the Netherlands leads the EU in Internet penetration (94 % of the households) and broadband connections (38.4 per 100 inhabitants).

Maintaining this investment-friendly reputation is a high priority for the Dutch government, which provides public information and institutional assistance to prospective investors through the Netherlands Foreign Investment Agency (www.investinholland.com). Additionally, an EU format information gateway, www.answersforbusiness.nl, is readily accessible for information on regulations, taxes and investment incentives that apply to foreign investors in the Netherlands.

V. India and The Netherlands: Natural Business Partners

Indian investment in the Netherlands

As per figures of the Dutch Central Bank, in 2014, Indian investments to the Netherlands were Euros 2.376 billion and total Indian investments (cumulative) during the period 2004-14 were Euros 11.840 billion. The Netherlands is the fifth largest investor in terms of foreign direct investment into India with FDI inflows during period April 2000 to December 2016, amounting to US $ 19.81 billion (accounting for 6% of total inflows into India) (Embassy of India, The Hague, the Netherlands). According to Reserve Bank of India (RBI), the Netherlands was the third largest investor in India during the financial years 2012-13, 2014-15 and 2015-16 and fourth largest investor during the financial years 2013-14 and 2016-17.

Box: 2 Why Indian companies should consider trade and investment with the Netherlands

Over 170 million consumers (roughly one-third of the population of the expanded European Union of 28 Member States) reside within a 300-mile radius of Rotterdam.

It is a highly outward oriented economy with merchandise trade accounting for close to 80 percent of the Netherlands' GDP.

The Netherlands is a key center within the global business network with an advanced infrastructure geared towards the transportation of goods, people, and electronic data.

It's core distribution points include Rotterdam, Europe's largest port, and Amsterdam Schiphol Airport, the fourth largest airport in Europe.

The Netherlands has capitalized on its location and advanced economy to become one of the top trading countries in the world.

The Netherlands is the sixteenth largest economy in the world and the fifth largest in the European Monetary Union (the Eurozone), with a gross domestic product (GDP) of $771 billion in 2016.

The Dutch economy is currently considered to be experiencing stable growth, and the IMF (World Economic Outlook, October 2017, IMF) projects economic growth of 3.1 percent of GDP in 2017 and 2.6 percent in 2018. Projected drivers of growth include increased exports and business investments, as well as newly invigorated domestic consumption.

Direct tax regime in Holland is geared to attract foreign investment and to foster entrepreneurship. With a competitive corporate income tax rate in Europe—20% on the first €200,000 and 25% for taxable profits exceeding €200,000—as well as many attractive incentive programs, wide tax treaty network, certainty in advance of future tax positions and special measures for highly skilled expats etc., the Netherlands offers a supportive fiscal climate for international companies. Holland offers a
India has consistently maintained bilateral trade surplus with the Netherlands over the last few years and was close to U.S. $ 3 billion during 2016-17.

In terms of trade and investment, India has strong economic interests in the Netherlands, which is at present the fifth largest investor of FDI into India. India's total trade (export plus imports) with the Netherlands amounted to U.S. $ 7 billion in 2016-17 and constituted just 1 % of India's total trade turnover. The trade balance continues to be in favour of India. India's total trade with Netherlands after reaching a peak of close to $13 billion in 2012-13 has been on a downward slide and fell to about U.S. $ 7 billion in 2016-17. During 2016-17, India's bilateral merchandise trade with Netherlands totaled $7 billion, consisting of $5 billion in Indian exports to, and $2 billion in imports. India's exports to the Netherlands fell from a peak of U.S. $ 10.6 billion (3.5% of India's total exports) in 2012-13 to U.S. $ 5.0 billion (1.8% of India's total exports) in 2016-17.

Focus needs to be on restoring and reviving India's exports to the Netherlands which is a gateway to EU. The Port of Rotterdam forms an important entry point for Indian exports and accounts for around 25% of Indian exports to the European Union. Trade and investment cooperation is a key component of India- However, there is potential for further growth in the trade relations. The Netherlands is home to a number of multinational and other companies, many of which have their production sites and business operations in India. It is also a source of useful technical know-how, besides FDI, in a variety of sectors – water management, upgrading of ports and airports, dredging, agro-processing, telecommunication, energy, oil refining, chemicals, and financial services. India's exports to the Netherlands have fallen from U.S. $ 10.6 billion in 2012-13 to less than half at U.S. $ 5.0 billion in 2016-17; over the same period imports from the Netherlands into India also fell from U.S. $ 2.4 billion to U.S. $ 1.9 billion.

Table:3 India Netherlands (NDLDs)Merchandise Trade (U.S. $ Million)				
Year	Exports to NDLDs	Imports from NDLDs	Total Trade	Trade Balance
	(1)	(2)	(1) +(2)	(1) -(2)
2000-01	880 (2.0)	438 (0.9)	1318 (1.4)	442
2006-07	2675(2.1)	1158 (0.6)	3833 (1.2)	1517
2009-10	6398 (3.6)	2130 (0.7)	8528 (1.8)	4268
2012-13	10565 (3.5)	2379 (0.5)	12944 (1.6)	8186
2013-14	7996 (2.5)	3139 (0.7)	11135 (1.5)	4857
2016-17	5070 (1.8)	1896 (0.5)	6966 (1.1)	3174

Figures in parenthesis indicate percentage in total exports/imports
Source: Import Export Data Bank, Government of India, Department of Commerce

Commodity profile of India's trade with the Netherlands

India's export basket to the region is diversified spread over 14 broad commodity groups accounting for about two-third of the total exports to the Netherlands. Diversified nature of India's export basket has lent resilience to India's exports to the Netherlands, but Indian exports have yet to carve out a niche in the Dutch market. Some of the important items with export share of commodity to the total exports to the Netherlands during 2016-17 (indicated in the parenthesis) were: petroleum refinery products (28%), engineering goods comprising mechanical & electrical appliances and transport equipment (13%), ready-made garments (8%), organic chemicals (7%) and pharmaceuticals (3%).

Table: 4 India's Exports to the Netherlands (in U.S. $ Million)			
Product	**2006-07**	**2016-17**	**CAGR**
1.Marine products	8 (0.3)	107 (2.1)	29.6
2.Rice	10 (0.4)	47 (0.9)	16.7
3.Tea	10 (0.4)	17 (0.3)	5.4

4.Coffee	5 (0.2)	7 (0.1)	3.4
5.Spices	4 (0.1)	20 (0.4)	17.5
6.Edible fruits & nuts	124 (4.6)	163 (3.2)	2.8
7.Petroleum products	697 (26.1)	1408 (27.8)	7.3
8.Pharmaceuticals	47 (1.8)	141 (2.8)	11.6
9.Organic Chemicals	119 (4.4)	350 (6.9)	11`.4
10.Leather articles	47 (1.8)	96 (1.9)	7.4
11.Readymade garments	294 (11.0)	395 (7.8)	3.0
12.Mechanical appliances	102 (3.8)	153 (3.0)	4.1
13.Electrical goods	71 (2.7)	224 (4.4)	12.2
14.Transport equipment	37 (1.4)	232 (4.6)	20.2
13.Sub total (1 to 12)	1575(58.9)	3360 (66.3)	7.9
14.Residual	1100 (41.1)	1710 (33.7)	4.5
Total exports to NDLDS	2675	5070	6.6
India's Total exports	126414	275852	8.1
Source: Import Export Data Bank, Government of India, Department of Commerce Figures within parenthesis indicate percentage share of product to total exports to Africa; CAGR-compound annual growth rate			

India's imports from the Netherlands are confined to a few products with engineering goods accounting for 35 % of the total imports from the Netherlands. A significant item within the engineering goods is ships and floating structures for the offshore oil industry. These accounted for more than 11 % of the total imports from the Netherlands.

Table: 5 India's Imports from the Netherlands (in U.S. $ Million)			
Product	**2006-07**	**2016-17**	**CAGR**
1.Chocolates	1.5 (0.1)	9 (0.5)	19.6
2.Organic chemicals	190 (16.4)	170 (9.0)	-1.1
3.Pharmaceuticals	10 (0.9)	31 (1.6)	12.0
4.Iron & Steel	128 (11.1)	103 (5.4)	-2.1
5.Aluminium refined	12 (1.0)	89 (4.7)	22.2
6.. Mechanical appliances	116 (10.0)	185 (9.8)	4.8
7.. Electrical goods	52 (4.5)	137 (7.2)	10.2
8.. Transport equipment	4 (0.3)	12 (0.6)	11.6
9.Ships & floating structures	154 (13.3)	210 (11.1)	3.2
10. Optical& precision instruments.	66 (5.7)	111 (5.9)	5.3
Subtotal (1 to 18)	733.5 (63.3)	1057(55.7)	3.7
Residual	424.5 (36.7)	839 (44.3)	7.1
Total imports from Netherlands	1158	1896	5.1
India's total imports Share %	185735	385356	7.6
Source: Import Export Data Bank, Government of India, Department of Commerce Figures within parenthesis indicate percentage share of product to total imports CAGR-compound annual growth rate			

- **Dutch-Indian trade is still small**

Trade flows between India and the Netherlands have increased over the years, but are still rather small, considering the size of the Indian economy. Twenty-nine countries worldwide import more goods from the Netherlands than India. For every Indian container arriving at a Dutch port, there are over twenty-five arriving from China. Indian and Dutch exports generally consist of different products. India is strong at low-skill labour-intensive products and IT-related services. The two countries experience little competition from each other on world markets. India ranks 30th among Dutch import partners, with a share of 0.6% in total goods imports. About half of Dutch imports from India are re-exported, mainly to other EU countries.

- **Trade in services**

Up to now, Dutch firms are not engaged (what about Shell, DSM, Philips?) in off-shoring specific services to India at a substantial scale. The principle motive for Dutch firms to invest in India is to gain a foothold in the fast growing Indian consumer market. If the Indian economy expands and the domestic market becomes increasingly open to foreign competition, Dutch investments in India will continue to rise. Meanwhile, Indian firms will also expand their overseas activities.

India has a strong position in the services trade and has increased its strength in recent years. This is reflected in increased openness of the services sector and a relatively high and increasing share of services in total trade of goods and services. Although the share of trade with India in total Dutch services trade is below 1%, the Netherlands rank within the top ten of industrialized countries trading services with India. Currently, India is mainly exporting computer services to the United States. However, given its revealed comparative advantage in computer services, India's export of computer services to the EU countries, including the Netherlands, may rise in the near future.

Indian businesses in the Netherlands

The Netherlands possesses a number of strengths that make it attractive to Indian companies wanting to enter the European market. The strengths of the Netherlands are, amongst others: geographical location, good infrastructure, a favourable fiscal climate, logistical expertise, technological know-how, flexibility, broad language skills and an internationally-oriented society. In the field of infrastructure, the port of Rotterdam plays a key role as an international transport hub, and so a key role in economic relations between India and the Netherlands, and the EU as a whole.

The Netherlands is steadily becoming an attractive destination for investments from India and figures amongst the top destinations. There are over 200 Indian companies having a presence in the Netherlands. These include all the major IT companies such as TCS, HCL, Wipro, Infosys, Tech Mahindra, NIIT, etc. Other prominent companies include LT Foods, Synthite, Sun Pharmaceuticals, Tata Steel, Kirloskar Brothers, Dr. Reddy's Labs, Dishman Chemicals, Aurobindo Pharma, Jindal Polyfilm, Cyient, etc. Major acquisitions in the Netherlands by Indian companies were: Tata Steel acquired the Anglo-Dutch Corus for US $ 7.6 billion; Apollo Tyres acquired the Dutch tyre maker VredesteinBanden and; The Serum Institute of India acquired the Dutch Bilthoven Biologicals which has given it access to technology and expertise for making the Injectable Polio Vaccine (Salk). Recently Amity Group has also set up an International school in Amstelveen. Many Indian companies are exploring the possibilities for further tie-ups.

Netherlands Foreign Investment Agency (NFIA): First point of contact for Indian companies

The Netherlands Foreign Investment Agency (NFIA) established more than 40 years ago, is an operational unit of the Dutch Ministry of Economic Affairs. The NFIA helps and advises foreign companies on the establishment, rolling out and/or expansion of their international activities in the Netherlands. The NFIA works together with Dutch embassies, consulates-general, and other organizations representing the Dutch government abroad, as well as with a broad network of domestic partners. NFIA (https://investinholland.com/)

- Facilitates preliminary in-person meetings and provide up-to-date, personalized information;
- Offer personal guidance and counseling, starting in the country of origin;
- Arrange contacts with relevant business partners, government authorities, a variety of Dutch networks and service suppliers, and other relevant contacts;
- Organize customized fact-finding trips together with network of regional economic development partners;
- Present concrete solutions that simplify and optimize establishment in the Netherlands;
- Offer special services such as:
    - Logistics Matchmaking Service (with NDL/HIDC);
    - Tax ruling practice for large foreign investors (with Tax Inspectorate and

Ministry of Finance);

  - Knowledge Migrant Facility for new foreign investors (with IND/Immigration & Naturalization Service)
  - Orange Carpet Visa Facility (with relevant consular departments).

- Support preservation and further enhancement of a favorable Dutch investment climate;
- Deliver advocacy towards national and EU governments;

Box 3: Helping Companies Locate in the Netherlands Since 1978

The Netherlands Foreign Investment Agency (NFIA) is proud to celebrate 40 years of rolling out the orange carpet for companies. Since 1978, NFIA has served as a one-stop-shop for successful European expansion, supporting more than 4,000 companies from some 50 countries to establish or expand their business in the Netherlands.

Dutch Trade Network in India Celebrating 40 years of NFIA

Invest in Holland Network

Regional Partners of the Invest in Holland network are:

- Northern Netherlands
- East Netherlands
- Flevoland
- Utrecht
- North Holland
- **amsterdam inbusiness**
- South Holland (THBA)
- **South Holland (Rotterdam)**
- **South Holland (InnovationQuarter)**
- Zeeland
- **Brabant Development Agency**
- Limburg

Highlighting four of our critical regional partners for India:

amsterdam inbusiness (aib)

Amsterdam Inbusiness is the official foreign investment agency of the Amsterdam Metropolitan Area, which includes Amsterdam, Amstelveen, Almere and Haarlemmermeer. Amsterdam Inbusiness assists foreign companies with the establishment and expansion of their activities in the Netherlands. They can help you create a convincing business case for setting up in the Amsterdam Metropolitan Area by offering practical advice and relevant information.

https://www.iamsterdam.com/en/business/setting-up/our-services/about-us

BOM Foreign Investments (BOM)

When you relocate, set-up or expand your business, you need the essentials to be taken care of quickly and thoroughly. In the province of Brabant, BOM Foreign Investments is your partner every step of the way. It offers a comprehensive range of services and support- free of charge – on a wide range of subjects. Whether it be issues with building permits, finding new premises or sites for development, questions on employment law, understanding tax incentives or help business development and networking. Based in Tilburg BOM Foreign Investments is part of the Brabant Development Agency (BOM) made up of 100 highly specialized and motivated people. To facilitate foreign investments in Brabant, we combine our services with the unique expertise and support of our colleagues at BOM. This expertise includes supporting R&D programs and initiating and stimulating innovative industrial projects as well as support in financing privately. **More information: https://www.investinbrabant.com/**

InnovationQuarter

InnovationQuarter (IQ) is the Regional Development Agency for the province of South Holland. IQ has a dedicated foreign investment team in place to facilitate foreign companies in finding the right locations and facilities for setting-up or expanding business in this region. IQ provides tailor-made assistance and can connect you with key network contacts, especially in sectors such as Life Sciences & Health, Cleantech, Security, Horticulture, Smart Industry and Maritime. Services are provided on a confidential basis and free of charge. For more information: www.innovationquarter.nl.

Rotterdam Partners

Rotterdam Partners helps your business to make a running start. From A to Z, Rotterdam Partners will help you do business in Rotterdam and provide strong and comprehensive support to both local and international investors with all the information necessary to set up or expand their business as efficiently as possible. The Rotterdam Expat Centre will help expats feel at home in the Netherlands. All services are free of charge and confidential. More information: www.www.rotterdampartners.nl

VI. India as a strategic market for Dutch investors

India is becoming a strategic market for Dutch companies. The most significant strategic reasons for Dutch companies to operate in India are expected future economic development, the size of India's domestic market and the demands of customers to operate in India. The business climate in India is both rewarding and challenging.

India's ambitious and innovative flagship programmes like Make-in-India, Digital India, Skill India, Smart Cities, Clean India, Clean Ganga, Start-up-India, etc. provide ample complementarities and opportunities for Indo-Dutch cooperation going forward. These have made a tremendous impact on business and investment climate in India. India continues to be among the top ten countries in terms of FDI inflows globally and the fourth in developing Asia, as per the World Investment Report 2017 by the United Nations Conference for Trade and Development (UNCTAD). India's FDI inflows have increased to $44.5 billion in 2016 making it the **10th** largest recipient of FDI inflows as compared to $24.2 billion in 2012. The Netherlands received more **than two** times India's FDI inflows at U.S. $92 billion in 2016. Dutch business and investors are well positioned to seize the early mover advantage and be a part of the resilient and strong India growth story. The Netherlands was the third largest contributor of FDI outflows in the world. These were of the order U.S. $ 174 billion in 2016.

There exist huge investment opportunities in life sciences and water management for Dutch companies in India. Some of the sectors include:

Horticulture & propagation materials: Floriculture production in India is stimulated by the growing purchasing power of Indian consumers and the resulting demand for more variety and quality. There is good scope for Dutch companies to participate in production, agents, or distributors. So far, Dutch companies are primarily active in the production of vegetable seeds.

Life sciences & health: On the one hand India must cope with the constant threat of infectious disease, on the other hand the concern for modern, lifestyle-related, non-communicable diseases is increasing. Rising proportion of all deaths are caused by chronic illnesses such as cardiovascular diseases, cancer, and diabetes.

Water: India is a large nation with many water-related problems. Of these flooding, drought, and an uneven distribution of water sources are the most significant. The Ministry of Water Resources is the governmental body responsible for water management in India. Dutch companies can participate in collaborative projects targeted at monitoring flooding, dam safety, hydraulic structures, and water quality.

Dutch companies in India

All relevant Dutch business sectors and almost all Dutch multinationals are represented in India. **There are more than 200 Dutch companies already present in India.** Major Dutch companies like Shell, Unilever, Akzo Nobel, DSM, Philips, KLM and Rabobank have a presence in India. Dutch SMEs with niche technologies and world-class expertise are also actively looking at the Indian market .

VII. Dutch industrial strength-core industries and clusters

Netherlands: an Agri-food Powerhouse

Second only to the U.S. for agri-food exports (Euro 82.4 billion exports in 2015) worldwide. The Netherlands boasts more than 4,150 companies in this key sector — from farm to fork. In fact, 12 of the world's largest agri-food companies have major production or R&D sites in Holland, including Cargill, Heinz, Monsanto, Unilever, Mead Johnson, ConAgra, Mars and many more. Mars, an international company with more than 65,000 employees worldwide, has its biggest factory in Veghel, Brabant where it employs 1,200; Heinz' European Innovation Center in Nijmegen is the company's largest R&D center outside of the U.S. with 160 chefs, food scientists, quality engineers and researchers. Kikkoman began its modern-day connection with the Netherlands in 1997 with construction of its first European soy sauce plant and later opened an R&D facility in Food Valley.

Yuzaburo Mogi Honorary CEO & Chairman of the Board Kikkoman, *"We chose Wageningen because of the proximity of Food Valley and other research institutes and facilities. Here we can develop products that are particularly suitable for the European market".*

Fueled by world-class research institutes for food innovation, medical universities and numerous public-private partnerships between science, industry and government, the

Netherlands has the 2nd highest private R&D investment in agri-food in Europe. Resources range from Wageningen University and Research Centre—named the best global university for agricultural sciences according to U.S. News & World Report, 2016—to the Top syndicates for Knowledge and Innovation Agri-food (TKI Agri-food), which combines government, academic and private sector players to advance the Dutch agri-food sector—and the Dairy Campus, where parties across the entire dairy value chain are driving innovation and sustainable development. The Netherlands, long Europe's trading crossroads, is a smart choice to locate a pan- European operation — whether it's a European headquarters, a shared services center, a customer care center, a distribution and logistics operation, or an R&D facility.

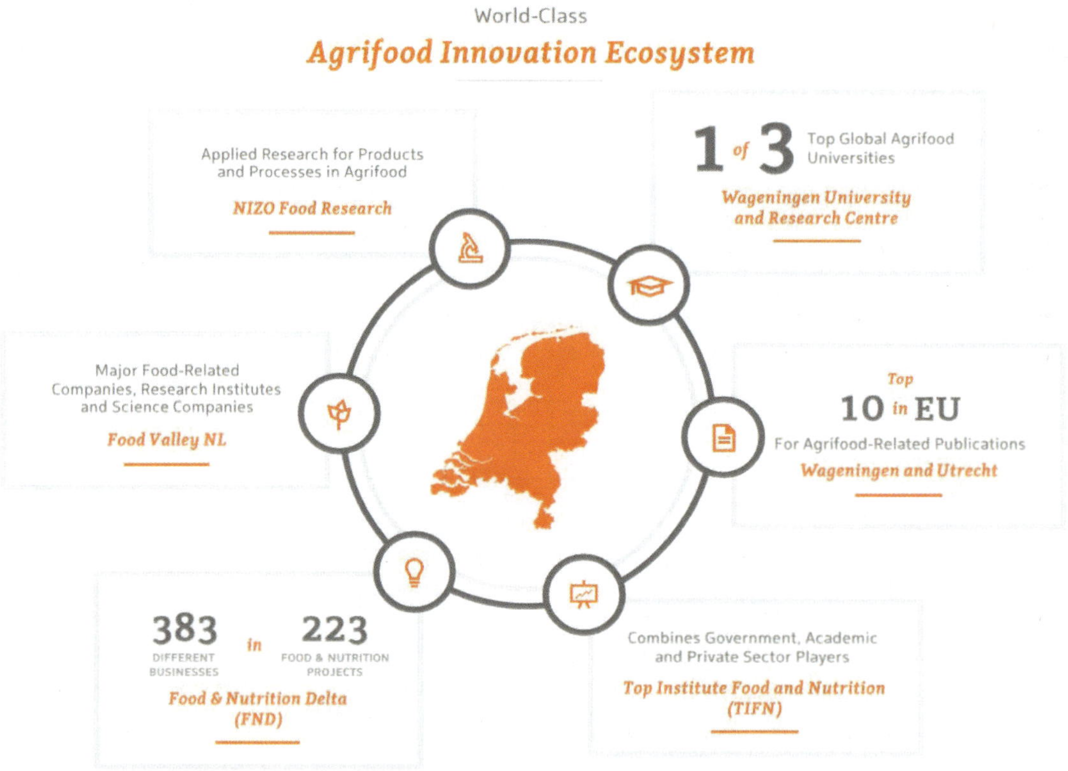

A Life Sciences & Health Hub

The Netherlands' contributions to medical technology date back to the invention of the microscope (1590) and the first functioning artificial kidney (1943). Home to more than 2,500 innovative life sciences and health companies and research organizations—including major multinationals like MSD, Amgen, Genmab, Astellas, Glaxo Smith Kline and Medtronic—the Netherlands has one of the most concentrated life sciences regions in the world. Medtronic choose the Netherlands for a multitude of operations, including R&D, headquarters, manufacturing and logistics. In fact, in the last three years, 17 major biotech deals involved Dutch companies. With a presence in the Netherlands for more than half a century, Abbott now employs 2,500 across the Netherlands. The company's Zwolle branch houses finance, planning and customer service operations, while its Breda location serves as the logistical heart of Abbott's worldwide operations. According to Jolanda Cortlever, General Manager, Zwolle & Breda Branches Abbott, *"We also have access to well-trained, multilingual staff who can work very well in Englis. The country is politically stable, while the financial climate and the tax regime and customs facilities are all to our benefit."*.

Fueled by world-class health and research institutes, including 12 research universities, 82 hospitals—eight of which are university medical centers—and a number of public-private partnerships (200 **plus** partners spanning 100 projects) between science, industry and government, some €2 billion is invested in R&D in this industry annually. **Netherlands ranks No.4 in patent application for medical technology worldwide**. Holland's high-quality infrastructure for clinical research, competitive tax support measures, pro-business climate and strategic location provide life sciences companies a springboard to the European market and an excellent environment for business expansion and acceleration. Its medical exports were of the order € 37 billion.

Information Technology (IT): The Digital Gateway to Europe

Holland's state-of-the-art, 100 per cent digital, advanced fiber-optic network and competitive fiscal climate support a strong community of startups and global IT companies. In fact, 60% of Forbes 2000 companies in the IT industry have already established operations in Holland. Unparalleled Resources for IT Companies with the highest broadband penetration per capita in the world—99% of all households—as well as one of the world's fastest average broadband speeds, Holland's IT infrastructure is one of the best on the planet.

Ranked **No. 3 on the 2017 Global Innovation Index (GII),** the Netherlands has a rich history of innovation. In fact, the Dutch invented Bluetooth, Wi-Fi, the CD and the DVD. Today, Holland's robust network of public-private partnerships, R&D ecosystems and education institutes ensure businesses have the resources they need to stay on the cutting edge of discovery.

A History of Innovation

Since landing in the Netherlands in 1924, New York-based technology and computing corporation IBM has grown to employ approximately 4,000 people there—making its Dutch presence almost as old and well-established as the company itself. Harry van Dorenmalen Chairman IBM, Europe has observed *"The Dutch have a focus on innovation and highly educated resources, which allow them to conduct groundbreaking research."*

Here in the Netherlands, global IT companies like Microsoft, Cisco, Interxion, **Infosys**, Huawei, Oracle, Intel, IBM, Verizon and Google tap into an unparalleled IT infrastructure, a competitive tax climate and a tech-savvy, English-speaking workforce. The Netherlands is also a hotspot for companies active in the global gaming industry — both serious and entertainment gaming — and is home to world-renowned gaming companies like Guerrilla Games, Perfect World, Kixeye and Activision Blizzard. In addition, the Netherlands has the largest security cluster and one of the most advanced markets of data centers in Europe—not to mention our world-class R&D facilities and logistics infrastructure—making the Netherlands a smart choice for any IT business operation.

Europe's Largest Startup Ecosystem

Renowned internationally for its open culture and emphasis on entrepreneurship and innovation, the Netherlands is home to a vibrant, collaborative startup ecosystem. **In fact, the Netherlands ranks No. 1 in the European Union for its startup business climate, according to the European Digital Forum's 2016 Startup Nation Scoreboard.** Holland's unrivaled digital infrastructure, highly educated, tech-savvy, English-speaking workforce and open corporate business culture provide an attractive and supportive test market for new business. **In the Netherlands it just takes 4 days to start a business as compared to 6 days each in the U.K. and Ireland and 10 days in Switzerland and more than two weeks in Germany. Ranked No. 4 in the EU on the 2017 European Innovation Scoreboard, the Netherlands is home to more than 10 leading innovation hubs, where startups benefit from world-class incubators and R&D facilities.**

As of 2015, a new regulation makes it possible for ambitious entrepreneurs outside of the European Union to apply for a temporary residence permit for the Netherlands. **The so-called "start-up visa" affords ambitious entrepreneurs one year to launch an innovative business. A prerequisite is that this start-up must be guided by an experienced mentor that is based in the Netherlands.** After one year, the start-up entrepreneur may have the duration of their residence permit extended based on the Dutch government's self-employment scheme. The Dutch government also offers tax incentives to promote corporate R&D and innovation, making the Netherlands one of the best values in Europe for startups.

Box 4: The Netherlands: The center point of the European startup

The Netherlands has traditionally been a country that welcomes entrepreneurial spirits. After centuries of enterprise and ingenuity, the combination of innovation, trade and entrepreneurship remains a driving force within the nation's economy and is a key source of economic renewal and job creation. As such, it is recognised that entrepreneurs stimulate economic growth.

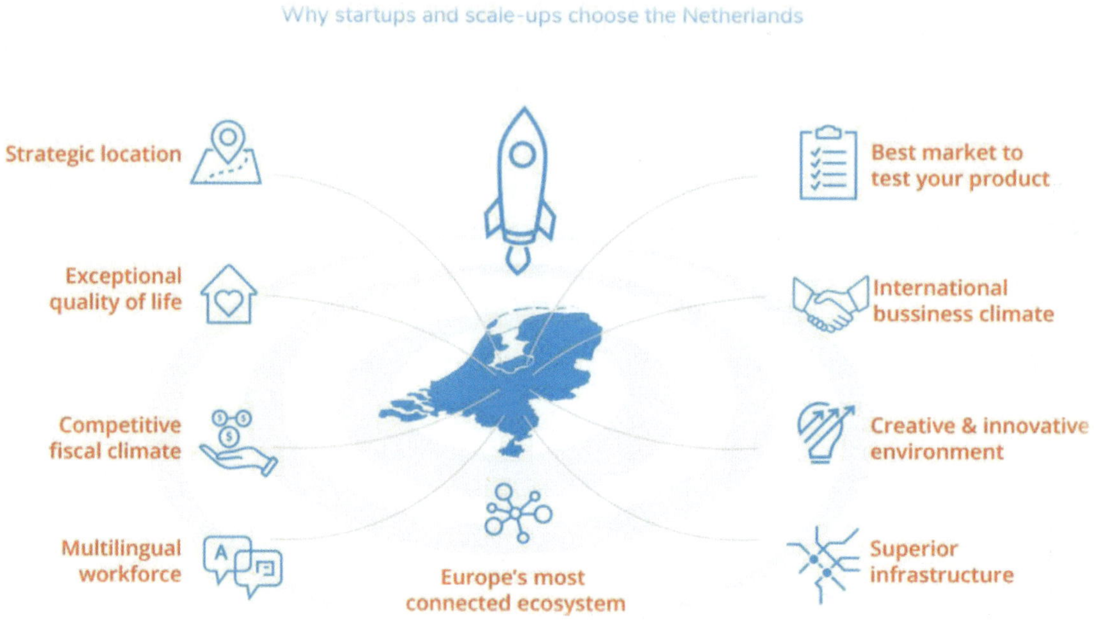

Few facts about Amsterdam's Startup:

- Leading tech giants choose Amsterdam for their European headquarters or development teams: Tesla, Uber, Optimizely, Netflix, Atlassian and Nextdoor.
- Amsterdam is the centre point for growth hacking: Growth Tribe Academy has educated over 1,400 people so far, while an abundance of bootstrapped scale-ups – including Usabilla, Squla, WeTransfer – prove that Amsterdam lives and breathes growth.
- Amsterdam is home to Europe's biggest startup incubator and co-working space.
- Amsterdam hosts an abundance of accelerators: Startupbootcamp – the leading startup accelerator outside the US – for ecommerce, fintech & cyber security and Smart City & living , Rockstart, Let it Grow, Open House, ACE Venture Lab, Fashion for Good and many more.
- Amsterdam has the most well-connected startup and tech ecosystem that collaborates via the Startup Amsterdam programme, with over 35 initiatives and projects that push for

more skilled talent, capital, launching customers, content and a more startup-like environment.

- Amsterdam's corporates form a powerful player in the ecosystem: Startup Amsterdam Corporate Network consists of 80+ corporates that act as sponsors, mentors or launching customers for startups.
- The local government acts as a launching customer themselves! Thanks to the Startup in Residence programme, not only can startups work with the municipality of Amsterdam on innovative urban solutions for the city, but civil servants receive training on Lean Startup, the Business Model Canvas and Growth Hacking to better understand the startup mentality.
- Amsterdam has an abundance of local talent thanks to a variety of tech academies: there are over 250 data science courses under one roof at Amsterdam School of Data Science, 20+ startup & coding academies, various upskilling programmes and four main universities with 100,00 students overall. We're even bringing coding classes to primary schools via Coding for Amsterdam.

Amsterdam is always buzzing with activity: 900+ yearly events, from meetups to conferences, that everybody can find on StartupAmsterdam's Event Calendar.

Europe's Energy Hub

The Netherlands is a leader in offshore, renewable and smart energy due to its progressive policies, affinity for innovation and environmentally conscious population. Committed to strengthening its already strong position in the global energy industry, the Netherlands offers world-class R&D facilities and outstanding incentive programs that support and stimulate energy innovation.

- **Offshore Energy:** Strategically located on the North Sea, the Netherlands is home to oil majors and maritime engineering multinationals servicing the North Sea Continental Shelf and far beyond. The Port of Rotterdam—Europe's largest harbor—plays a major role in Holland's off-shore energy success with one of the largest refining and chemicals clusters in the world. With access to workforce training institutes such as the Energy Delta Institute, Holland is also home to some of Europe's best engineering talent in the energy sector.
- **Renewable Energy:** The Dutch government offers a variety of competitive incentives to stimulate energy innovation and promote corporate use of renewable energy sources. As a result, the Netherlands has strengthened its top position in renewable energy R&D, particularly in wind turbine technology. This is further enforced by strategic public-private partnerships and world-class facilities, such as

the Top consortium for Knowledge and Innovation Offshore Wind (TKI Wind op Zee), the Energy Research Center of the Netherlands (ECN) and Delft University of Technology—one of the world's leading specialists in sustainable energy.

- **Smart Energy:** The Dutch government has invested heavily in smart grid innovations and solutions, facilitating developments in electric vehicles and smart energy technology. The Netherlands is home to the first 'live' smart grid community in Europe—Power Matching City in Groningen—as well as the second largest fleet of plug-in electric vehicles in the world after Norway.

Cyber Security

With the highest broadband penetration per capita in the world — 99% of all households—as well as one of the world's fastest average broadband speeds, the Netherlands is one of Europe's most-wired and cyber-secure countries. It also directly links continental Europe to North America, with most transatlantic sea cables going directly to the Netherlands. Google runs two data centers in the Netherlands, one of which is powered by 100% renewable energy.

Holland's state-of-the-art, 100% digital, advanced fiber-optic network supports an innovative community of startups, data centers and multinational digital companies including Microsoft, Cisco, Tata, Infosys, Huawei, Oracle, Intel, IBM, Verizon and Google. Amsterdam, in particular, has become a digital hub in recent years thanks to the presence of AMS-IX: the world's leading Internet exchange point.

Plus, Holland's world-class resources and dynamic startup climate are drawing in an expanding array of providers and helping to steadily decrease tariffs and further improve cost competitiveness, making the Netherlands one of the best values in Europe.

Logistics and Distribution

The Netherlands is an open economy. The country has a long-standing tradition of international trade and it has become an important player in the world economy as a result. The Netherlands is a hub for foreign-owned logistics and distribution operations. In fact, Holland is the true gateway to Europe and home to some 900 distribution centers of North American and Asian companies.

Driven by world-class seaports, centrally located airports and an extensive, modern network of roads and highways, Holland's logistics infrastructure and presence of top-notch logistic service providers is a major asset to companies looking to establish international logistics/distribution operations in Europe.

The Netherlands' strong position in terms of logistics is due to the favorable geographic location of the country in the heart of Europe, a sound infrastructure that includes the Port of Rotterdam, the Port of Amsterdam, Amsterdam Schiphol Airport and a sophisticated logistics sector. This is reflected in the World Bank Logistics Performance Index 2016 where the Netherlands is ranked fourth. The Netherlands came out on top in terms of the efficiency and effectiveness of its Customs and other border procedures, the quality of its transport and IT infrastructure for logistics, the ease of use and affordability of its shipping, and the level of professionalism in the Dutch logistics industry.

Add to that Holland's supportive corporate tax structure, highly educated, multilingual workforce, robust supply chain and advanced network of suppliers and it's no wonder major multinationals like Coca-Cola, IBM, Huawei and Tommy Hilfiger choose the Netherlands as their logistics and distribution gateway to Europe to manage their supply chain or grow their e-commerce operations. The direct added value of the port of Rotterdam in 2015 (last known figures) was more than 12 billion euro. The direct and indirect added value came to almost 21 billion euro. This represents 3.1% of Dutch gross domestic product (GDP) (Port of Rotterdam Statistics). **It handled 461million tonnes of cargo throughput in 2016 and was ranked number one in Europe and ninth globally. It also handled more than 12 million TEUs in 2016. The port of Rotterdam is the largest container port in Europe. Even the largest vessels can enter the port 24/7 due to the large depth and no restrictions from tides or locks.**

The Port of Rotterdam is Europe's largest port by far. More than 1,000 American and Asian companies have centralized their European distribution activities from the Netherlands. The country hosts over 19 million square meters of distribution centers (about 3,000 football/soccer fields). The Netherlands makes extensive use of IT to deliver optimal supply chain solutions in time-critical areas like food and cut flowers. The country is a pioneer in the development of environmentally sustainable logistics and 'silent' logistics. The Netherlands has a close-knit network of canals and rivers which is extremely well-connected to other forms of transport. The customer, a shipper or haulier for example, is offered an integrated solution to his transport needs.

Box 5: Matchmaking Services for logistics partnership in Europe

Holland International Distribution Council (HIDC) – Dutch: Nederland Distributieland (NDL) – is a private, non-profit organization providing matchmaking services for logistics partnerships in Europe.

HIDC represents the Dutch logistics sector, and helps international companies make a smooth entry into the European market through the region's leading gateway, the Netherlands.

- HIDC provides the answers to European supply chain challenges.
- Regulatory compliance is an essential component of international trade.
- With that in mind, HIDC helps companies use their own strengths to maximize their benefits.
- A solid and transparent supply chain ensures hassle-free operations within the EU.

Furthermore, HIDC advises large and smaller companies on ways to minimize costs of supply chain operations in the European market.

All advisory services are free of charge, totally confidential and without any obligation. HIDC works closely together with the Netherlands Foreign Investment Agency, an operational unit of the Dutch Ministry of Economic Affairs and Climate. Their offices are located in North America, Asia and Europe.

For more details, please visit https://hollandinternationaldistributioncouncil.com/en

- **Logistics performance**

There is no better way to access mainland Europe than through its front door - the Netherlands. The country's strategic location, highly developed transportation infrastructure, efficient customs authorities, and logistics professionals are enough reasons for foreign companies to grow and expedite their international operations. The Netherlands is a densely populated country which makes its transport modes the busiest in the world. This intensive demand commands a high degree of quality. The Dutch infrastructure ranks second in the World's Bank Logistics Performance Index (Table: 7). As the logistics distribution hub of Europe, the Netherlands has known for many years how to maximize the speed and efficiency of transporting goods. And what's more, customers in Northwest Europe can be reached within 24 hours, according to logistics operators.

The Dutch logistics market is one of the most mature and established in Europe. To a large extent, this is due to the gateway function the Netherlands has for the European continent. From the so-called ‘mainports‘ in the west of the country – mainly Schiphol Amsterdam Airport and the Port of Rotterdam - to the consumer markets on the European continent a strong clustering of distribution centers has formed. The main triggers for this are the fact that the Netherlands has a well-developed infrastructure and is geographically well placed to service many of the main consumer markets of Europe. Other important factors include the multilingualism of the population and the positive business environment, which includes a well-developed logistics industry, a flexible customs regime and relatively low corporation taxes. As a result, many companies that provide transport, logistics and related services are established in the Netherlands.

Trade logistics are a key to trade efficiency, integration into global value chains and economic growth. Good logistics lower trade costs boost competitiveness and improve export performance. Inefficient and insufficient trade logistics deprive domestic firms of their competitive advantages along the way between the factory and the buyer. Logistics have changed drastically over the past two decades. The “made in the world” notion of having parts of a product made in different countries and by different producers in one country underlines the need to deliver raw materials, spare parts and final products to producers around the world in a timely manner. The rise of the just-on-time production model, where manufacturers keep low levels of inventories and depend to a large extent on timely delivery of supplies, has increased the importance of logistics. A good logistics chain can facilitate higher economic growth, business competitiveness and infrastructure services in quality and quantity. A good example of non-tariff barriers is the cost of transporting products to foreign markets, in pecuniary terms (freight costs) and in terms of delays in moving goods.

The Logistics Performance Index (LPI) published by the World Bank every two years is based on a worldwide survey of operators on the ground (global freight forwarders and express carriers), providing feedback on the logistics “friendliness” of the countries in which they operate and those with which they trade. LPI captures the efficiency of logistics services in several dimensions and provides an estimate of the supply chain performance using an average scale (from zero to five) that weighted the country scores on six key dimensions: The index ranges from 1 to 5, with a higher score representing better performance. Overall LPI score is the weighted average of the country scores on the six key dimensions. Netherlands is ranked 4th globally out of 160 countries ranked while India is ranked 35th**.** The index is based on six areas (i)**Customs:** Efficiency of the clearance process (i.e., speed, simplicity and predictability of formalities) by border control agencies, including customs; (ii)**Infrastructure**: Quality of trade and transport related infrastructure (e.g., ports, railroads, roads, information technology); (iii)**International Shipment**: Ease of arranging competitively priced shipments;(iv)**Logistics Competence:** Competence and quality of logistics services (e.g., transport operators, customs brokers); (v)**Tracking and tracing:** Ability to track and trace consignments; and (vi)**Timeliness:** Timeliness of shipments in reaching destination within the scheduled or expected delivery time. The compilation of the index is primarily through an online survey that of around 1,000 professionals in international freight forwarding. It is important to know that the evaluations come from respondents outside the country being evaluated, so the responses reflect a country's logistics friendliness as it is perceived by logistics professionals from abroad. LPI relies on the freight forwarders' perception of performance, along the six objective dimensions. As such it remains a subjective, rather than a wholly objective, assessment of logistics performance. The LPI provides some insights on the cost of logistics to country competitiveness—and the sources of those higher costs., viz, efficiency of the customs clearance process, quality of trade and transport related infrastructure, ease of arranging competitively priced shipments; competence and quality of logistics services, ability to track and trace consignments and frequency with which shipments reach the consignee within the scheduled or expected time. All global logistics service providers operate European Distribution Centers (EDCs) in the Netherlands. As a consequence, the logistics sector is a very important contributor to the Dutch economy.

Table: 6 International LPI Scores and Rankings

Country	Overall	Customs	Infrastructure	International Shipments	Logistics Quality and Competence	Tracking and Tracing	Timeliness
Germany	4.23 (1)	4.12 (2)	4.44 (1)	3.86 (8)	4.28 (1)	4.27 (3)	4.45 (2)
Luxembourg	4.23 (2)	3.90 (9)	4.24 (43)	4.24 (1)	4.01 (10)	4.12 (8)	4.80 (1)

Sweden	4.20 (3)	3.92 (8)	4.27 (3)	4.00 (4)	4.25 (2)	4.38 (1)	4.45 (3)
Netherlands	4.19 (4)	4.12 (3)	4.29 (2)	3.94 (6)	4.22 (3)	4.17 (6)	4.41 (5)
India	3.42 (35)	3.17 (38)	3.34 (36)	3.36 (39)	3.39 (32)	3.52 (33)	3.74 (42)
China	3.66 (27)	3.32 (31)	3.75 (23)	3.70 (12)	3.62 (27)	3.68 (28)	3.90 (31)
Connecting to Compete 2016 Trade Logistics in the Global Economy The Logistics Performance Index and Its Indicators							

One of the main drivers of the strong logistics cluster in the Netherlands is the presence of a high-quality, dense infrastructure for all transport modes. The Port of Rotterdam and Schiphol Amsterdam Airport are key elements in this network. The Dutch road infrastructure is a dense network of over 2,500 kilometres of motorways, providing direct access to virtually all major cities and towns in the country. Access to Germany in the east and Belgium in the south is easy and direct, especially for road transport originating in the Port of Rotterdam. The quality of the infrastructure is good and traffic güidance and safety have a high priority. In addition to the motorway network, the Dutch waterways are important transport routes. The Netherlands is located at the estuaries of three major rivers, which are extended by numerous artificial waterways such as the Amsterdam-Rhine Canal. As a result, the Netherlands is characterized by a large proportion of freight that is transported over water, an impressive 45% of all Dutch cargo transport in terms of tone/kilometer. The Port of Rotterdam has long been the largest in the world, and is still the largest European seaport. In addition, the Port of Amsterdam can be counted as a major European bulk port. A number of inland container terminals have been developed, particularly in the south of the country, to support container transport by water.

Schiphol Amsterdam Airport is one of the major air transport hubs in Europe. It handled 64 million passengers, about 1.6 million tonnes of airfreight and reached almost 479,000 air transport movements in 2016 (Schiphol Group, 2016). In addition, the regional airports of Rotterdam, Eindhoven, and Maastricht-Aachen play an increasingly key role, particularly with passenger traffic. Eindhoven and Maastricht have recently emerged as extra locations for airfreight handling in the Netherlands. It must be noted that this often involves handling of airfreight trucked in from Schiphol and other European airports.

- **Shipping connectivity-Netherlands number one in Europe**

Access to world markets depends to a large extent on the availability of regular and efficient maritime transport connections, especially liner shipping services. UNCTAD's Liner Shipping Connectivity Index (LSCI) aims at capturing a country's level of integration into the existing liner shipping network by measuring liner shipping connectivity. Since 2004, UNCTAD's Liner Shipping Connectivity Index (LSCI) has provided an indicator of each coastal country's access to the global liner shipping network. The complete time series is published in electronic format on UNCTAD stat (UNCTAD stat, 2016). The LSCI is calculated as the weighted average of five core components that capture the deployment of container ships by liner shipping companies to a country's ports of call: (a) the number of ships; (b) their total container carrying capacity;(c) the number of companies providing services with their own operated ships; (d) the number of services provided; (e) the size (in TEU) of the largest ship deployed. Most overseas trade in manufactured goods is moved in containerized regular "liner" shipping services, and the LSCI reflects a country's connection to global networks of such services. The LSCI can thus help traders, investors, port operators and policymakers in their assessment of a country's position within such global networks, both as regards changes over time, and in comparison, to neighbouring countries. When interpreting the LSCI, it must be borne in mind that a country's liner shipping connectivity is closely related to its seaborne trade in manufactured goods. A low value in the LSCI reflects that there are fewer and smaller ships deployed on fewer services by fewer companies. This lower level of deployment is usually the result of (a) a country's geographical position; (b) its trade volumes; and (c) its ports' attractiveness to shipping lines. **Table 8** gives trends in LSCI for top seven countries and India. ***The country with the highest LSCI scores in 2017 is China with a score of 167, the Netherlands LSCI at 86, is ranked sixth globally and number one in Europe in terms of LSCI.*** The LSCI score of a country is not only determined by its trade volume, but increasingly by its position, i.e. its degree of connectivity within the global liner shipping network.

Table: 7 Liner Shipping Connectivity Index (LSCI) Maximum 2004:100							
Country (Rank)	**2004**	**2008**	**2013**	**2014**	**2015**	**2016**	**2017**
China (1)	100.00	137.38	156.19	157.51	165.05	167.13	167.48
Singapore (2)	81.9	94.5	106.9	113.2	117.1	119.5	115.1
Korea, Republic (3)	68.7	76.4	100.4	108.1	113.2	112.6	109.9
Hong Kong, China (4)	94.4	108.8	116.6	116.0	116.8	100.5	105.4
Malaysia (5)	62.8	77.6	98.2	104.0	110.6	102.5	98.1
Netherlands (6)	78.8	87.6	87.5	94.2	96.3	84.4	86.4
Germany (7)	76.4	89.3	88.6	94.0	97.8	89.8	85.9
India	34.14	42.18	41.29	44.35	45.61	45.85	46.24

- **Trading Across borders**

Trading across Border Indicators of the World Bank, which to a large extent capture the degree of cross-border trade facilitation. There is great variation in time and cost to export/import a container across the world. Trading across Border Indicators of the World Bank, which to a large extent capture the degree of cross-border trade facilitation. **The ease of trading across borders rankings puts the Netherlands at number one vis-à-vis 146 ranks of India**. Sixteen of the 28-member countries including Netherlands are ranked number one globally on this parameter. **The Netherlands, ranked 1st globally in terms of trading across borders, where it takes just one hour and no cost to export a container and 1 hour and no cost to import a container in terms of time and money spent on border and documentary compliance.** In contrast, in India, it takes 144 hours or 6 days and $ 474 to export a container in fulfilling border and documentary compliance and 326 hours or close to two weeks and $ 678 to fulfill border and documentary compliance for importing a container.

Table: 8 Netherlands Trading Across Borders Time & Cost Indicators								
	Export				**Import**			
	Time to Export In Hours		**Cost to Export in U.S. $**		**Time to import In Hours**		**Cost to import in U.S. $**	
Country	**BC**	**DC**	**BC**	**DC**	**BC**	**DC**	**BC**	**DC**
Netherlands (1)	0.0	1.0	0.0	0.0	0.0	1.0	0.0	0.0
EU average (14)	8.1	1.4	85.2	17.0	1.7	1.1	29.2	4.5
OECD	12.7	2.6	149.9	35.5	8.7	3.9	111.6	25.7
East Asia	55.9	68.1	387.6	112.1	70.5	65.6	431.1	111.5
India (146)	106.1	38.4	382.4	91.9	264.5	61.3	543.2	134.8
Note: BC-bordercompliance;DC-documentcompliance;figures within parenthesis global rank								

California-based Tesla designs and manufactures EVs, as well as EV powertrain components for partners such as Toyota and Daimler. Tesla has delivered more than 2,400 Roadsters to customers worldwide.

Tesla Motors have opened a Distribution Center in Tilburg, Netherlands as a key step towards beginning worldwide distribution of Model S, the world's premium sedan. This new facility will serve as Tesla's European service and parts headquarters, as well as the final assembly and distribution point for Model S vehicles sold in Europe. Tesla has located the new European Distribution Center in Tilburg almost two years of on-going cooperation between Tesla, BOM Foreign Investments, NFIA (Netherlands Foreign Investment Agency), CBRE Group, Inc. and the City of Tilburg.

General production of European left-hand drive Model S is planned to begin in March 2013.

Tesla's new 62,000 square foot facility is centrally located to enable efficient, timely and cost effective operations throughout Europe. Starting this month, the new distribution center will begin stocking parts for both the Tesla Roadster and Model S. In addition to parts warehousing, Tesla plans to utilize this facility for vehicle importing operations, final vehicle assembly and distribution, service headquarters, technical training operations, parts remanufacturing, collision repair and more. The new Tesla European Distribution Center will lead to the creation of approximately 50 jobs in the next few years.

Tesla's goal is to accelerate the world's transition to electric mobility with a full range of increasingly affordable electric cars.

VIII. Holland: Industrial Policy Framework

Incentives for industry

Industry-specific, targeted investment incentives have long been a well-publicized tool of Dutch economic policy to facilitate economic restructuring and to promote energy conservation, regional development, environmental protection, R&D, and other national socioeconomic goals. Such subsidies and incentives are available to foreign and domestic firms alike and are spelled out in detailed regulations. Subsidies are in the form of tax credits that are usually disbursed through corporate tax rebates or direct cash payments in the event of no tax liability. Since 2011, successive Dutch governments have pursued a targeted stimulus program for nine sectors. The stated ambitions for this policy are to improve the Dutch role in knowledge-intensive industries to reach a top 5 rank among global knowledge-based economies by 2020; to increase the percentage of R&D efforts to 2.5% of GDP by 2020; and, to establish Innovation Consortia wherein both public and private sectors participate with a budget over €500m. In a joint effort with academia and the private sector, Dutch government has instituted preferential policy that releases over a €1billion in additional funding for R&D and product innovation in the following top sectors in the 'business economy'/private sector:

1. **Agriculture and Food:** is the third largest top sector in terms of turnover, €73B, and employs the largest number of self-employed, 91,000.
2. **Chemical Industry:** accounts for nearly 8% of production and consists of companies with a large number of employees. Three quarters of the sector is focused on innovation, more than the other sectors.
3. **Creative Industry**: nearly 97,000 different firms are active in this sector, but in economic terms it generates 2% of private sector production.
4. **Energy:** a capital-intensive sector with few firms, production (€55B) and investments (€5B) are very high.
5. **High tech systems and materials:** the largest Top Sector by production, added value and export. Highly committed to innovation, this sector accounts for nearly half of the R&D efforts made in the Netherlands.
6. **Life sciences & Health:** this sector contains the fewest number of firms, just over 2,000, but represents nearly 13% of Dutch R&D investments.
7. **Logistics:** one of the most important sectors of the Dutch economy, accounting for 11% of production (€126B), 10% of all added value in the Netherlands and 12% of employment.
8. **Horticulture and propagation materials**: this sector is characterized by the large export component, as nearly three quarters of production (€21B) is sold abroad.
9. **Water:** this sector consists of the subsectors maritime production, drinking water, and delta engineering. It generates 2.2% of Dutch GDP, but it contributes nearly 9% of all R&D investments (€468m).

Nearly a quarter of all firms in the Netherlands are active in one of these Top Sectors, which generate 21% of overall employment, account for 27% of value added, and represent 38% of total Dutch production. These sectors are also highly export-orientated, accounting for 40% of Dutch exports. Over 95% of R&D expenditures on proprietary research within the Netherlands take place in these Top Sectors. In the coming years, more funding is expected to be available as additional government policies in taxation, SME support, and product development are rolled out. By 2015 the government share in the national Top Sector program is expected to amount to €2billion.

Foreign investors are free to apply for government grants as the Dutch government reviews applications on a case-by-case basis with no preference for nationality of the bidder. Although much coordination of investment support is executed at the Ministry and NFIA level, the Netherlands has a strong tradition of regional development agencies. These agencies advise both business and local authorities on the best use of regional development funds. Many of these have evolved into investment agencies that provide equity participation for up-and-coming enterprises in the region. Also, funding from the EU for regional development is distributed through the regional development agencies. Regional non-tax incentives are available in the form of cash grants, low interest loans, and local government participation and export guarantees for selected areas.

The Netherlands has no formal foreign investment screening mechanisms, and no foreign ownership quotas, with the exception of certain limitations in the strategic sectors (*transportation, energy, defense and security, finance, postal services, public broadcasting, and the media.*) There is also no requirement for nationals to have an equity stake in a Dutch-registered company.

Corporate Governance

The rules on acquisition, mergers, takeovers, and reinvestment are nondiscriminatory. The Social Economic Council (SER), an official advisory body of government, business, and labor representatives, administers Dutch M&A rules. SER rules are intended, first and foremost, to protect the interests of stakeholders and employees. They include requirements for the timely announcement of M&A plans and for discussions with trade unions.

A corporate governance code of conduct took effect in 2004 aimed at improving transparency in shareholder/management relations, as well as the structure and accountability of management. The voluntary Corporate Governance Code is monitored by a Committee on Corporate Governance, which can also propose adjustments to the Code in areas such as executive salaries, risk management, shareholders rights and responsibilities.

There are no restrictions on the conversion or repatriation of capital and earnings (including branch profits, dividends, interest, royalties), or management and technical service fees, with the exception of the nominal exchange license requirement for nonresident firms.

Expropriation and Compensation

The Netherlands maintains strong protection on all types of property, including private and intellectual property, and the right of citizens to own and use property. Expropriation of corporate assets or the nationalization of industry requires a special act of parliament, as seen in the nationalization of ABN Amro during the 2008 financial crisis. In the event of expropriation, the Dutch government follows customary international law, providing prompt, adequate compensation and ample process for legal recourse.

Dispute Settlement

Dutch contract law is based on the principle of party autonomy/full freedom of contract. Signing parties are free to draft their agreement in any form, any language, based on the legal system of their choice.

Dutch corporate law provides for a legal and fiscal framework that is designed to be flexible. This element of the investment climate makes establishment in the Netherlands especially attractive to foreign investors. Since January 1st, 2013, further liberalization of corporation law has been implemented that allows for even more flexibility in corporate governance structure, legal entity of the enterprise and governance of holdings. **The Dutch civil court system has a special chamber dedicated to business disputes, the Enterprise Chamber. This feature is unique among EU member states** and the Enterprise Chamber has received positive reviews from institutional investors, companies and investors around the world. Enterprise Chamber judges include experts in commercial fields as well as the legal profession. They have proven their ability to act swiftly and decisively in a wide range of corporate disputes, including conflicts regarding corporate control.

As a member of the International Center for the Settlement of Investment Disputes (ICSID), the Netherlands accepts binding international arbitration between foreign investors and the state. The Netherlands is one of the initial signatories of the New York Arbitration Convention (UNCITRAL) and permits local enforcement of arbitration judgments decided in other signatory countries.

Performance Requirements and Incentives

There are no trade-related investment performance requirements in the Netherlands. General requirements to qualify for investment subsidy schemes apply equally to domestic and foreign investors. **There are no requirements for employment**

of local capital or managerial personnel. In practice, however many chief executives of major U.S. subsidiaries in the Netherlands are Dutch or other EU nationals. This is because highly professional managers are available at a cost less than that of posting an American abroad.

Right to Private Ownership and Establishment

There are full rights of private ownership and establishment of business enterprises in the Netherlands, except in some cases in the strategic sectors. Legal guidelines on mergers, acquisitions and reinvestment are applied without regard to nationality.

Thirteen of Fortune 500 companies have global headquarters in the Netherlands, and another 16 have located their Euro Zone headquarters in the Netherlands. Of the 400,000 registered companies in the Netherlands, nearly 6,000 enterprises are 100 per cent - owned by foreign firms. Most of these have EU origins, but outside the EU area the U.S. is the most important country of origin: approximately 20% of foreign owned enterprises in the Netherlands are American. Although they amount to 1% of the total number of firms in the Netherlands, foreign owned companies account for nearly 15% of employment in the business economy.

Protection of Intellectual Property Rights

- **IPR:** The Netherlands has a generally strong set of laws and regulations that protect intellectual property rights (IPR). With the implementation of EU Directive 2004/48 on the enforcement of intellectual property rights, IPR holders have more instruments at their disposal to enforce their rights in civil court. The Netherlands is a member of the World Intellectual Property Organization (WIPO), has signed on to the Paris Convention for the Protection of Industrial Property, and conforms to accepted international practice for the protection of technology and trademarks.
  Despite its participation in the negotiations on the Anti-Counterfeiting Trade Agreement (ACTA) treaty, the Netherlands has not yet signed this treaty in its current form. The EU has requested the European Court of Justice to advise on the compatibility of ACTA with existing European treaties, in particular with the EU Charter of Fundamental Rights.
- **Copyright:** The Netherlands has implemented the European directive 98/44/EC in 2006, bringing domestic legislation in line with the WIPO 1996 Copyright Treaty (WCT) and the WIPO Performance and Phonogram Treaty (WPPT). There is

consensus among policy makers on the need for measures aimed at raising awareness of IPR rules and regulations and to strengthen enforcement.

- **Patents:** The Netherlands is a signatory to the European Patent Convention, which provides for a centralized Europe-wide patent protection system. This convention has simplified the process for obtaining patent protection in EU Member States. Infringement proceedings remain within the jurisdiction of the national courts, which could result in divergent interpretations. The single, harmonized European patent procedure will allow for easier application in just three languages. This so-called unitary patent will be under jurisdiction of a single European patent court to adjudicate disputes.

  Patents for foreign investors are granted retroactively to the date of the original filing in the home country, provided the application is made through a Dutch patent lawyer within one year of the original filing date. Dutch patents are valid for 20 years. Legal procedures exist for compulsory licensing if the patent is inadequately used after a period of three years, but these procedures have rarely been invoked. Patent applications can be filed in English, but the conclusion must be written in Dutch.
  Beside the possibilities civil action, all IPR laws contain penal bylaws and reference to the Criminal Code. In 2012, parliament passed legislation that strengthens the oversight and coordination of seven different collective institutions that concern themselves with the control, administration and remuneration of commercial use of works under IPR holder ship. The Dutch government has recognized the need to protect intellectual property rights, and law enforcement personnel have worked with industry associations to find and seize pirated software. Dutch IPR legislation currently in place explicitly includes computer software as intellectual property under the copyright statutes.

Transparency of Regulatory System

Laws and regulations that affect direct investment, such as environmental rules, and health and safety regulations, are non-discriminatory and apply equally to foreign and domestic firms. As an EU member and as a Eurozone country, the Netherlands is firmly integrated in the European regulatory system with national and European institutions exercising authority over specific markets/industries, consumer rights and competition behavior of individual firms.

In 2013, the new Authority Consumer and Market (ACM) succeeded the three separate market regulators for Consumer Protection (Consumenten Autoriteit), Post and Telecommunications (OPTA) and Market Competition (NMA).

Financial markets are regulated by the central Bank DNB and the Financial Market authority, AFM, in an interconnected EU and national system of prudential and behavioral oversight. Their EU counterparts are ECB and ESMA.

Efficient Capital Markets and Portfolio Investment

The Netherlands is home to the world's oldest stock exchange – established four centuries ago – and to Europe's first options exchange, both located in Amsterdam. The Amsterdam financial exchanges are part of the NYSE/Euronext group that operates stock exchanges and derivatives markets in Amsterdam, Brussels, London, Lisbon, New York and Paris.

Dutch financial markets are fully developed and operate at market rates, facilitating the free flow of financial resources. The Netherlands is an international financial center for the foreign exchange market and for Eurobonds and bullion trade. The flexibility that foreign companies enjoy in conducting business in The Netherlands extends into the area of currency and foreign exchange. There are no restrictions on foreign investors' access to sources of local finance.

State-Owned Enterprises (SOEs)

There is very little state intervention in the private sector, and little or no direct or indirect state support is provided to industry. The state's equity stake in (former) state owned enterprises has been decreasing for decades. The Dutch government maintains an equity stake in a small number of enterprises and some ownership in companies that play a key role in strategic sectors. Government-controlled entities maintain dominant positions in gas and electricity distribution, rail transport, and the water sector. The government nationalized ABN AMRO Bank and ASR insurance company in 2008 due to the global financial crisis. In February 2013, it nationalized the bank and insurance company SNS Reaal (since re-named Volksbank) due to the bank's steep losses in its real estate portfolio. In November 2015, ABN AMRO regained its status as a publicly-traded company. The Netherlands has an extensive public broadcasting network, which generates its own income through advertising revenues but also receives government subsidies. For a complete list of all 34 government owned entities, please see https://www.rijksoverheid.nl/onderwerpen/staatsdeelnemingen/vraag-en-antwoord/in-welke-ondernemingen-heeft-de-overheid-aandelen.

Corporate Social Responsibility

The Netherlands is a global leader on corporate social responsibility (CSR). Principles of CSR are promoted and prescribed through a range of corporate, governmental and international guidelines. In general, companies closely guard their reputation for CSR, and consumers are increasingly opting for products and services that are less harmful to animals and the environment.

As adherents to the OECD Guidelines for Multinational Enterprises, the Dutch Ministry of Economic Affairs houses the National Contact Point (NCP) that promotes the Guidelines and helps mediate any concerns that persons, NGOs and enterprises may have regarding the implementation of the OECD Guidelines by a specific company. (For more information, visit www.oecdguidelines.nl)

Dutch firms comprise 2% of the Dow Jones World Sustainability Index, which represents the top 10% of leading sustainable companies in the world in every industry. When specified for Eurozone companies, Dutch firms comprise over 10% of the most sustainable enterprises. Of the nineteen 'super sectors' identified by the Dow Jones Sustainability Index, four sector leaders are Dutch: Akzo Nobel (Chemicals sector), UniLever (Food and Beverage), Philips (Personal and Household) and KLM/Air France (Travel and Leisure).

Labour

The Netherlands has a strongly regulated labor market (nearly 85% of labour contracts fall under some sort of collective labor agreement), comprised of a well-educated, multilingual, and motivated workforce. Legislation has been passed or is in progress to increase labour market flexibility. Labour/management relations in both the public and private sectors are generally good in a system that emphasizes the concept of social partnership. Although wage bargaining in the Netherlands is increasingly decentralized, there still exists a central bargaining apparatus where labour contract guidelines are established.

The terms of Collective Labour Agreements apply to all employees in that sector, not only the union members. To avoid surprises, potential investors are advised to consult with local trade unions to determine which, if any, labour contracts apply to workers in their business sector prior to making an investment decision. Collective bargaining agreements negotiated in the past few years have, by and large, been accepted by the rank and file without much protest, despite only moderate wage increases. Days lost to strikes are relatively few.

The Dutch economy derives its strength from free trade and a stable industrial climate fostered by partnership among unions, employers' organizations, and the government. There is substantial labour involvement in corporate decision-making on matters affecting workers. Each company in the Netherlands with at least 50 workers is required by law to institute a Works Council, with which management must consult on a range of issues including investment decisions. Because of sustained economic growth in recent years, unemployment had been decreasing until mid-2009, when the effects of the financial crisis set in. The annual average unemployment rate was estimated 4.3 % during 1999-2008 in comparison to 8.7 % in the Euro Area, but at 5.9 % in 2016 it remains well below EU average of 10% (WEO, October 2017, Statistical Appendix). The working population consists of 7.9 million persons. Workers may be found through government-operated labor exchanges, a rapidly growing number of private employment firms, or through direct hiring.

Foreign-Trade /Free Trade Zones

The Netherlands has no free trade zones (FTZs) or free ports in the sense of territorial enclaves where commodities can be processed or reprocessed tax-free. However, FTZs exist which are reserved for bonded storage, cargo consolidation, and reconfiguration of non-EU goods. In this regard, the Dutch economy has a very large component in the area of transport, transit, logistics and distribution. Dutch customs authorities oversee a large number of customs warehouses, free warehouses and free zones along many of the Netherlands trade routes and entry points.

Schiphol Airport alone handles over 1.5 million tons of goods for distribution. Specific premises in the Schiphol area is designated a customs-free Zone. The Port of Rotterdam is Europe's largest seaport by volume, handling over 37% of all cargo shipping on the Le Havre – Hamburg coastline, and processing over 442 million tons of goods in 2012. Many agents operate customs warehouses under varying customs regimes on the premises of the Port of Rotterdam

IX. The Netherlands: Global competitiveness & Innovation

The Global Innovation Index (GII)

Global Innovation Index (GII) is calculated as the average of two Sub-indices. The innovation Input Sub-Index gauges elements of the national economy which embody innovative activities grouped in five pillars (i) Institutions; (ii) Human capital and research;(iii) Infrastructure;(iv) Market sophistication; (v) Business sophistication. The innovation Output Sub-Index captures actual evidence of innovation results, divided in two pillars ;(vi) Knowledge and technology outputs and; (vii) Creative outputs.

The Netherlands ranks No. 3 on the 2017 Global Innovation Index (GII). As one of the world's most innovative countries, Holland outpaces the U.S., the U.K., Ireland, Germany, and more. Each year, the GII surveys 127 economies using dozens of metrics that provide a high-level look at innovative activity. India is ranked 60th worldwide on GII. Its 81 indicators explore political environment, education, and infrastructure and business sophistication. The GII is co-authored by the World Intellectual Property Organization (WIPO), Cornell University and French graduate business school INSEAD. In addition to ranking No. 3 overall on the GII, the Netherlands ranks first in the following categories: business sophistication, knowledge absorption, intellectual property payments, ICT services imports, and FDI net outflows. Furthermore, Holland has strengths in human capital and research, infrastructure, market sophistication, and knowledge, technology and creative outputs, indicated the GII. Besides ranking highly on the GII, the Netherlands leads other indexes such as the European Innovation Scoreboard and has innovation hubs across the country.

Global Competitiveness

Since 2005, the World Economic Forum has published the **Global Competitiveness Index (GCI)**. The GCI combines 114 indicators that capture concepts that matter for productivity and long-term prosperity. These indicators are grouped into 12 pillars: institutions, infrastructure, macroeconomic environment, health and primary education, higher education and training, goods market efficiency, labor market efficiency, financial market development, technological readiness, market size, business sophistication, and innovation. These pillars are in turn organized into three sub-indexes: basic requirements, efficiency enhancers, and innovation and sophistication factors. The three sub-indexes are given different weights in the calculation of the overall Index, depending on each economy's stage of development, as proxied by its GDP per capita and the share of exports represented by raw materials. The GCI includes statistical data from internationally recognized organizations. **The Global Competitiveness Report 2017–2018 has ranked the Netherlands at 4th out of 137 countries. The Netherlands has maintained its position with the support of a strong education system and high levels of tech readiness among businesses and individuals.** The Dutch economy remains one of the most sophisticated and innovative in the world, with an open and efficient goods market. Its thriving innovation ecosystem, ranked 6th globally, puts the country in an excellent position to shape the unfolding Fourth Industrial Revolution. **China is the highest ranking among the BRICS group of large emerging markets, was ranked 27th and India 40th.**

Competitiveness within Europe

The Netherlands is the third most competitive nation in the European Union according to the 2014 World Economic Forum's *Europe 2020 Competitiveness Report*. The Netherlands has overtaken Denmark while moving up one place on the index from 4th in 2012 to 3rd in 2014. The new ranking can largely be attributed to strong performances in the areas of smart and inclusive growth fuelled by an impressive university system, high levels of social inclusion and a robust ICT sector. It is based on indices to track the progress of EU member states according to the themes smart growth, sustainable growth and inclusive growth. These three axis form the backbone of the research and focus on pertinent issues relevant to the well-being of European citizens, including creating dynamic economic opportunities, promoting resource efficiency and enhancing social and territorial cohesion. Based on the three overarching themes, the index is further divided into seven pillars, each with their own indicators, which are deemed vital to growth and job creation. These seven pillars are: (1) **Enterprise environment** addresses opportunities for businesses, industry cluster development, entrepreneurship and access to finances;(2) **Digital agenda** includes ICT readiness, ICT usage and ICT impact (access to services, patents, business model creations).;(3) **Innovative Europe** refers to expenditures on research and development (availability of scientists/engineers, cited scientific articles, university-industry collaboration, etc..;(4) **Education and training** examines the quality and accessibility of the education system;(5) L**abour market and employment** looks at labour market efficiency and labour participation; (6) S**ocial inclusion** addresses issues related to the accessibility of healthcare, social safety nets and opportunities for social mobility; and;(7). E**nvironmental sustainability** surveys issues of natural resource use and efficiency. These factors are then assigned scores mined from a World Economic Forum database covering 148 countries to form the Europe 2020 Competitiveness Index. The ranking is then determined by weighing the averages of factors composing these pillars (a value from one to seven), with higher values indicating better performance in that area.

The Netherlands' ranking of third overall is a telling sign that the Dutch continue to be high performers in terms of both economic growth and social progression in Europe. Placing third overall in the areas of smart growth and inclusive growth, the society thrives due to a world-class education system (2nd overall), willing and innovative use of ICT (1st overall), a friendly business environment (3rd) and a high-level of social inclusion (2nd).

Table: 9-Netherlands Ranking in select Global Indicators

Parameter	Year	Global Rank
Logistics Performance Index (LPI), The World Bank	2016	4th (1st)
Liner Shipping Connectivity Index (LSCI), UNCTAD	2017	6th (1st)
Trading across borders	2017	1st (1st)
Global Innovation Index (GII), World Intellectual Property Organization	2017	3rd (3rd)
Global Competitiveness Index, World Economic Forum	2017-18	4th (2nd)

Note: Figures within parenthesis indicates rank within Europe

X. Insights and observations from leading Indian companies operating in the Netherlands

Apollo Tyres

Apollo Tyres Ltd, acquired the 100-year-old Vredestein Tyres business in the Netherlands 7 years ago, Its European headquarters are located in Amsterdam and Research & Development centre is located in Enschede, The company has gone from strength to strength. Its state-of-the-art facility serves as a hub for the development and testing of car and van tires. In 2013, Apollo opened its global R&D center in Enschede with more than 100 R&D specialists from various parts of the world. This strategic acquisition by Apollo has brought gains in terms of tire technology, skilled resources, brand value and a well-established distribution network. The strategy of using Vredestein's network to stake a claim in the highly-competitive European market paid off and, as icing on the cake, the company was honored with the Tyre Manufacturer of the Year award, at the Tyre Technology International Awards for Innovation and Excellence 2013, in Cologne, Germany.

In the words of **Mr. Onkar S. Kanwar**, Chairman of Apollo:

"Our experience so far in the Netherlands has been extremely fruitful and we can say, without a doubt, that it is a country with a strategic vocational advantage, being in the heart of Europe. The business climate is progressive and welcoming. The people are very

friendly and open to innovation and change. All this adds up to an ideal business destination. Additionally, the Netherlands Foreign Investment Agency (NFIA) has been a very supportive business partner across various facets over the last several years. This has encouraged us and been a key factor in our decision to make further investments in the Netherlands."

HCL Technologies

With more than 110,000 people in 32 countries, HCL helps businesses become more lean and agile by providing them with IT services ranging from applications and infrastructure to engineering and R&D. HCL operates in industry sectors such as financial services, manufacturing, and telecommunications, and works with leading technology companies including Microsoft, Cisco, and Google.

In 2017, HCL has opened a new office in Amsterdam. Amsterdam is a natural choice, with its growing reputation as the emerging center for FinTech and startups – as well as being close to The Hague, is where HCL has a large digital customer experience lab. The choice was mainly inspired by the city's talented workforce and its proximity to some of HCL's key clients. In the words of Mr Sudip Lahiri, HCL's head of financial services for Europe, *"The purpose of this office is to be close to businesses, because Amsterdam is a business hub".* Mr Lahiri further added *"One key reason is the closeness to the talent pool. Not just experienced people, but also the young people. So that access to talent is very important for our business," he said. "And of course, most importantly, the access to our target customers who we'd like to engage with. They are all here."*

Cerexagri | UPL

Cerexagri is a fully owned subsidiary of United Phosphorus Ltd. (UPL), the leading global producer of crop protection products, specialty chemicals and other industrial chemicals. UPL today ranks amongst the leaders of the generic agrochemical companies in the world. Rotterdam has become its prime location for doing business in Europe. This subsidiary has a production capacity of 45,000 tonnes of crop protection products and has added to capacity in 2016. The facility also includes an R&D department aimed to enhance the efficiency of their business. The development lab is mostly engaged in the development and registration of plant protection products and the improvement and support of production processes. The R&D department consists of two co-operating groups, Product Chemistry and Chemical Formulators.

According to General Manager, Cerexagri, Mr André Langendoen, *"Cerexagri is based in Rotterdam because we can find well-trained staff here, we need those people in our product research and development"* continues André. *"Moreover, the advanced transport infrastructure allows us to ship our products from Rotterdam very quickly."* UPL recognizes the advantages of using the innovation-logistic synergy that the city offers to build their business in Europe. The Indian parent company refers to the cost-quality efficiency and the support offered by the central and local government authorities to be the key to further re-expand their activities in Rotterdam.

Tata Consultancy Services

TCS set up its European operations back in 1992, when it established it's Continental Europe Headquarters in Amsterdam. In the intervening period, the Netherlands region has become one of TCS' highest growth markets across Europe. TCS enjoyed consistent support from the local authorities in order to make the transition of its associates into the Netherlands as smooth as possible. This included facilities such as the Expat Center in Amsterdam, as well as the business and community events organized by Invest in Holland partner amsterdam inbusiness (aib).

Mr. Amit Kapur, Director & Head Benelux

For TCS, the Netherlands has always been, and still is, a major growth region reflecting the European trend. The company has achieved impressive double-digit growth, together with high margins and strong cash-flow, and continues to focus on pushing growth. The company has grown in stature, today serving some 350 European clients from 21 locations across Europe. In addition to this, TCS has fostered partnerships with over 200 academic institutions, impacting more than 15,000 young Europeans.

As one of the first technology companies of Indian origin to set up its offices in the Netherlands, TCS' engagement with the public authorities paved the way for many other companies that followed.

Wipro

Wipro Technologies is a global IT, consulting and outsourcing company with headquarters in India. Its 145,000 employees serve over 900 clients in 57 countries across the world. The southeast part of the province of Brabant is widely recognized as a center of innovation across a variety of sectors, including high tech, automotive and semiconductor industries. As a result, it is now known as the 'Brainport' of the Netherlands. This innovative culture, along with its strategic location between Rotterdam and major European markets, has helped to foster a thriving multi-national business community, which hosts 1,400 foreign companies employing 90,000 people.

Wipro worked closely with Brabant Foreign Investments (BOM) and the NFIA to set up their new service center. "These relationships were key to our success," said Timo. "The NFIA and BOM were very pro-active when it came to linking us with local institutions, business leads, potential partners, employees and networking opportunities."

Infosys

Opening of Infosys European Union Headquarter in Amsterdam

Infosys, a global leader in consulting, technology and next-generation services, has opened a new state-of-the-art office space in Amsterdam in September 2017. The investment in the new office represents Infosys' continued commitment to the Dutch market, as it endeavors to take its service offerings across Artificial Intelligence, automation, data and analytics, digital and platform technologies, to clients across sectors such as financial services, insurance, healthcare, and manufacturing.

The company currently has more than 20 clients in the country and employs over 1,100 people including those working at client locations in the Netherlands.

According to Rajesh Krishnamurthy, President and Head of Europe, Infosys: "The Netherlands is one of our largest markets in Europe and we are encouraged with the traction we have seen in the region. Over the past 15 years, Dutch clients and prospects have been keen adopters of new technologies and our strengthened presence in the market will enable our customers to embrace innovations such as Artificial Intelligence, automation and digital services, to help them achieve their growth and digital transformations ambitions."

Tata Steel

CEO of Tata Steel Europe, Mr. Hans Fischer, took to the controls of a pile-driver recently, to strike the first foundation pile into the ground at the company's steel plant in IJmuiden. In doing so he symbolically marked the start of a new 200-million-euro development phase at the site in the north of the Netherlands. The expansion sees the construction of a third continuous casting line at the IJmuiden plant for the production of high-tensile steels, including advanced high-strength steel and ultra-high-strength steel.

In a continuous casting machine, molten steel is poured directly into the casting machine then rolled out through a cooling process featuring rollers, to form slabs or large rolls.

Kirloskar Brothers

Kirloskar Brothers Limited is a world class pump manufacturing company with expertise in engineering and manufacture of systems for fluid management. Kirloskar Pompen BV (KPBV) Incorporated in 2008, is a subsidiary of Kirloskar Brothers Limited with its head office based in the Netherlands. The responsibilities are setting up distribution network in Europe, Marketing support for Distributors, Technical support such as: Engineering / Service and After service, Creation of Kirloskar brand in Europe and Stocking and assembly of pumps.

The key markets are Power, Water / Waste water and sewage, Industry, Irrigation, Distribution, Service and After service. Each of the served segment's market needs are shaped by the desire to procure quality products at reasonable prices. KBE is in the position to offer just that to their clientele, and the products must help their clients to better add value to their own end customers.

Kirloskar Pompen BV offers Service and after service throughout Europe together with its selected service partners in the region.

Serum Institute

Serum Institute of India Pvt. Ltd. I s currently the world's largest vaccine manufacturer by number of doses produced and sold globally. Serum Institute made its first international strategic acquisition, in 2012, when it acquired Bilthoven Biologicals from the Dutch government. The acquisition ensured access to technology and expertise for making the Inactivated Polio Vaccine. This furthered the Serum Institute's ambition to help achieve the worldwide eradication of Polio, by establishing an important manufacturing base in Europe. It also enhanced Serum Institute's offerings in the pediatric vaccine segment. On its choice of location, Serum Institute's Executive Director, Dr. Suresh Jadhav, stated: "*The Netherlands being very foreign-investor-friendly, proactive, and supportive in whatever way possible, was a major factor for Serum Institute's investment in the country.*"

From its European manufacturing facility, the Serum Institute accesses developed markets in Europe and USA for existing and future products currently in the development pipeline. Its focus is on innovative yet cost-effective solutions in new vaccines R&D, so as to address vaccine-related challenges for the benefit of the global population. Dr. Jadhav: *"Following our existing long-standing collaboration, the acquisition of the 40-acre Bilthoven Biological facility has further strengthened our position and boosted partnership in Indo-Dutch bilateral relations."*

Amity International School

Amity International School in Amsterdam

Amity Global Education Foundation from India has recently established a premium International School in Amstelveen just south of Amsterdam. Amity, established over 25 years ago has 150,000 students studying across 12 countries with over 1,000 acres of campuses, dozens of schools and Universities. Amity is one of the largest 'not-for-profit' education foundation in the world that offers education for children of 40 days old to Post-doctoral level in it's different campuses.

Amity International School Amsterdam has opened doors in February, 2018 for primary education and obtained International baccalaureate (IB) candidacy. School has established world class facilities for 175 students and plans to expand to 500 students by 2021, with grades all the way up to IB diploma.

Amity International School Amsterdam is the latest addition to Amity campuses spreading across India, London, Singapore, Dubai, Abu Dhabi, South Africa, Mauritius, China, New York and San Francisco.

The Amsterdam region is becoming an increasingly popular location for international companies, which also means a growing demand for places at international schools, where the children of those new employees will be educated. Having enough of these international schools is crucial to maintaining the region's attractive business climate, which is why local authorities have been working hard to open new schools and increase the capacity of the existing ones. The new Amity International School Amsterdam is helping to meet that need.

Choosing for the Amsterdam region

In March 2015, when academic delegation of Vrije university/VUmc (coordinated by Prof. Hari S. Sharma) as part of 'India Days mission' led by mayor of Amsterdam, HE Eberhard van der Laan visited the Amity University campus in Delhi and signing of the MoU between two universities for bilateral research and teaching cooperation. The follow up of the MoU began with the visit of Dr. Atul Chauhan, President Amity Global education in January 2016 when a clear need for an International school emerged after detailed discussions with various educational institutions and Amsterdam In Business partners as large number of children waiting to join international education. Stressing the need and commitments, then mayor of Amstelveen, HE Miriam Van't Veld offered all possible help to Amity in setting up an International school in the city of Amstelveen. In response to her, Dr. Chauhan stated 'please provide us a piece of land, we will built the best school of your country'. Search for land began that eventually ended at famous van Leer building that has now turned into a premier Amity International school.

"We've received a lot of support from the Amstelveen and Amsterdam municipalities," says Dr. Atul Chauhan, whose organization looked at many possible locations. "We are grateful to the Mayors, Deputy Mayors and directors for their backing." "Apart from helping us with the legalities and the bureaucratic part of it, we've received a very warm welcome in Amsterdam metropolitan."

"We have the best of both worlds here," says Dr Chauhan "We're twenty minutes away from the center of Amsterdam, and we have the Amsterdam Forest close by, so we've got absolutely beautiful surroundings in a wonderful family housing location."

International learning in Amsterdam and beyond

The school has obtained PYP candidacy status with the International Baccalaureate Organisation, which helps ensure consistency if a student relocates to another school. There is also a lot of space within the IB program to develop a unique curriculum. "We're trying to educate our children to be global citizens, who can integrate anywhere in the world. To support this, we have brilliant and dedicated teachers from around the globe, with great international experience. For more information, one can visit www.amityschool.nl

Tech Mahindra

Tech Mahindra Ltd, a specialist in digital transformation, consulting and business re-engineering has further extended its presence in Europe by inaugurating a new office space in Sweden in 2015.

According to Vikram Nair, President – Europe, Tech Mahindra " *Europe has been a strategic market and our business footprint spans across 20 countries in the region. We continue to invest in partnerships with niche and specialist vendors. Investing deeply in this region to create more job opportunities is also a reaffirmation of our long-term commitment*"

LT Foods

Inauguration of Plant of LT Foods Europe BV by Mayor of Rotterdam

LT Foods Limited is a branded specialty foods company. The company is engaged in milling, processing and marketing of branded and non-branded basmati rice, and manufacturing of rice food products in the domestic and overseas market. Its operations include contract farming, procurement, storage, processing, packaging and distribution. LT Foods' 12,000 sqm operation in Rotterdam will process brown rice for distribution within Europe. The arrival of LT Foods in Rotterdam is the result of collaboration between Rotterdam Partners, the Port of Rotterdam Authority and the Netherlands Foreign Investment Agency (NFIA).

Aditya Arora, Director of LT Foods Europe: observed *"We are setting up this plant in line with our growth strategy. It will strengthen our position in this segment and help us to expand our portfolio as well."*

Jet Airways

Mr. Vinay Dube, Chief Executive Officer, Jet Airways, H.E. Alphonsus H.M. Stoelinga, Ambassador of the Netherlands to India & Mr. Praveen Iyer, VP Commercial India Sales

Amsterdam Airport Schiphol's position as one of the largest gateways in Europe provides greater options for Jet Airways' freight customers, due to seamless links with sea, rail and road transportation. Jet Airways' direct daily flights from Amsterdam will benefit exports from the Netherlands including pharmaceuticals, specialized medical equipment, food and horticultural products, by facilitating access to Jet Airways' network across the vast Indian market. Jet Airways has also entered into a codeshare partnership with KLM Royal Dutch Airlines and Delta Air Lines to provide convenient connections for passengers to and from key destinations across Europe and North America via Amsterdam. The partnership will enable customers to enjoy enhanced connectivity and seamless travel throughout the combined networks of Jet Airways, KLM and Delta.

*"We are delighted to announce the launch of our new services to Amsterdam. India's trade relations with the Netherlands go back over 400 years and have continued to prosper in the modern age. The recent meeting between the Prime Ministers of India and the Netherlands has given a new impetus to this relationship. The new direct services by Jet Airways will facilitate greater engagement and co-operation between India and the Netherlands. As one of the fastest growing economies in the world, India has emerged as a key destination. Initiatives such as 'Make in India' and 'Startup India' launched by the Government of India have given a boost for foreign investment and trade" (*Mr. Naresh Goyal, Chairman, Jet Airways)

Associated Chambers of Commerce & Industry (ASSOCHAM)

Established in 1920, ASSOCHAM India has more than 450,000 members. ASSOCHAM, India assists its Indian members that want to expand abroad, and helps foreign companies that want to do business in India. ASSOCHAM India, the umbrella organization for Indian chambers of commerce, has set up its European office in Amsterdam.

According to Dr. Vikas Chaturvedi, the founder of ASSOCHAM Netherlands, the launch of ASSOCHAM's European base in Amsterdam *"will give a substantial boost in business between India and Europe. This will further enhance the role of the Netherlands as the gateway for Indian companies in Europe."* He added that *"Ascham's presence in Europe can act as a platform for European companies to enter into the Indian market very smoothly"*.

Launching of ASSOCHAM Netherlands by Mayor of Amsterdam

ICAI Netherlands Chapter: Boosting the Indo-Dutch Financial Corridor

Institute of Chartered Accountants of India (ICAI) set up its first European chapter at Amsterdam ,The Netherlands (Officially launched on 1st June 2017) . ICAI is the world's second largest accounting body. The event was inaugurated by CA Nilesh S Vikamsey: President of ICAI, Ms.Maaike Veeningen: Vice Mayor of Amstelveen and Shri Vijay Kumar Jaiswal: First Secretary of Indian Embassy.

According to Dr. Vikas Chaturvedi Founder and Chairman of ICAI Netherlands Chapter *"This set up will further enhance the brand building of CA profession in Europe, create network and job opportunities for CA's and boost bilateral business between India and Europe and in particular between India and the Netherlands".* According to Prashant Savla, Vice President of ICAI Netherlands Chapter & Finance Controller of Sun Pharma,*"By setting up European HQ in Amsterdam Area, Sun Pharma could attract good English speaking and well qualified workforce not only from Dutch market but also from rest of Europe and that too at a very reasonable cost"*

According to Himanshu Shah, Global Head of Compensation & Benefits, Koninklijke Vopak & Secretary of ICAI Netherlands Chapter, *"Despite its size, Netherlands is of strategic importance in many sectors within the European and global marketplace with its culture of innovation and entrepreneurship".*

Chartered Accountants based in the Netherlands with President of ICAI

XI. Interviews

H.E. Alphonsus Stoelinga, Dutch Ambassador to India, Dutch Embassy

"I see a surge in Dutch investments in India. PM Modi's flagship programs like Clean Ganga, 100 Smart Cities and Make in India are now really taking off –and are starting to attract Dutch companies. As these are multi-year investments, I expect many of these Dutch investments to be realized over the next five years"

- **Where do you see India-Netherlands relationship in next 5 years?**

I see a continuation of the surge in connectivity that we have witnessed in the past years. The Netherlands is now really becoming India's hub in Europe.

India's hub in Europe for exports: twenty percent of all Indian exports to Europe, enter Europe through the Netherlands. That represents a value of USD 10 billion (twenty percent of USD 50 billion). Can you imagine how many jobs we create in the ports and airport in the Netherlands?

And hub for investment: an increasing number of Indian companies consider the Netherlands as the ideal location for their European head office or distribution center. And since Brexit was voted in the UK referendum, the number of Indian companies establishing themselves in the Netherlands has more than doubled, creating thousands of jobs.

But the emergence of the Netherlands as India's hub in Europe for people to people contacts is the most remarkable. As you know AirFrance / KLM have signed a Joint Venture with Jet Airways. They work closely together and are integrating the business generated by the flights of Air France, of KLM and of Jet Airways between Europe and India and the business generated by all connecting flight of Jet Airways in India and of Air France and KLM in Europe. Add to that the connections between Europe and the US provided by Delta and the share that the group took in Virgin Atlantic and you have a business case that will give an edge to these airlines. Now – in May 2018- there are five times more daily, direct flight to the Netherlands than in May 2016. We see the results: my Embassy already issues every year 25 % more visa to Indians. In 2018 the visa the Netherlands issues to Indians will surpass the number issued to Chinese. No wonder we witness an increase in Indian students (up 100%) and of Indian tourists (up 20%) in the Netherlands.

To sum it up: in India- Netherlands connectivity the sky is not the limit.

Vice versa: the Netherlands is for India the third largest source of foreign direct investment and I see this trend prevailing over the coming years.

Then, the Netherlands is also India's hub for technologies:

Dutch companies are interesting partners for Indian companies, because of our technologies. Look at the agriculture sector and look at the ports, inland water ways and Ganga Rejuvenation Programme. And India is interesting for our companies because the USP of India is low cost innovation and smart scaling up of innovations. Why you think, all large Dutch corporations have R&D centers of thousands of engineers each in Bangalore, Delhi and Pune? I see a strengthening of this mutual profitable relationship.

Also, I see a surge in Dutch investments in India. PM Modi's flagship programs like Clean Ganga, 100 Smart Cities and Make in India are now really taking off –and are starting to attract Dutch companies. As these are multi-year investments, I expect many of these Dutch investments to be realized over the next five years.

- **What are the key sectors that you suggest Indian companies to look into The Netherlands?**

Here we have to make a distinction:

First we have the Indian investors who already have activities in Europe and wish to establish a head office or distribution center on the European continent. Or the Indian companies who wish to start exporting or are already exporting to Europe. To both categories we say: just compare the facts and figures and your choice for the Netherlands is a no brainer:

We are in the bulls eye of Europe, right in the center of UK, Germany and France and even with Britain outside the EU, it will be the Netherlands, closest to them (150 km) that will constitute the "Brexit bridge". In any case, I read that the Dutch authorities are already recruiting hundreds of custom officers for the port of Rotterdam for the post Brexit situation.

On top of that, the Netherlands has a favorable fiscal system, all people speak English and we have an open, egalitarian society.

Then we have the Indian investors that wish to take over companies in Europe or to do a greenfield investment on the continent. To them we say: the Netherlands is ranking the 4th most innovative economy in the World.

Innovative not only in technologies and IT, but also in governance, institutional and societal aspects.

I would exclude any sectors, but at the moment agro-food, life science and health and IT are the main targets of Indian investors in the Netherlands.

- **How has been your overall personal experience in last 6 years with regards to India-Netherlands relationship?**

I discovered that business relations in India are based on the parivar (family). With parivar I do not only mean the close relatives of the founder or owner of the company: I tell Dutch businessmen that, when you become part of the Indian company's parivar, when there is a relation between the Indian businessman's family members and the Dutch businessman's family members, when you attend -so to say- each other's shadi (marriages), then you become part of the family, of the parivar.

In that situation it is not the contact that defines the commitment of the Indian side. It is the contact, the personal contact, without the "R". And this mantra is valid for relations at the level of small SME's, but also at the level of the CEO's of huge corporations. I do not know why, but the Dutch fit perfectly in this Indian model. Like I do myself, by the way. Be part of the family.

- **Any particular USP of The Netherlands that you will like to highlight to Indian companies?**

We have spoken about the economic, the "hard" USP of the Netherlands.

Let's now turn to the "soft" aspects.

When an Indian company takes over a company in a foreign country, sooner or later it will have Indian staff employed in that country. And the Netherlands has proven to be a favorite destination for Indian families. First of course there is the language: even the street cleaners in the Dutch cities try to help you out in English. Many universities in the Netherlands have courses in English.

And you might run into one of the two and a half lakh Hindustani who live in the Netherlands.

And can you imagine: Amity University started a school for expatriate children. Then, it is safe to be at the streets in our cities, even for women, even in the night. The Dutch landscape is flat, as you know. But our society is also flat: the Dutch society is egalitarian: The children of the CEO have the same access to basic education and health services as the children of the driver of the CEO. Because government is responsible for health and education, both are of very high quality and reliability. For the Dutch themselves, but also for foreigners.

- **What advice/tips would you like to give to Indian companies that would like to set up their business in the Netherlands?**

First come to see us (or me) at the Netherlands Embassy in New Delhi, at the Consulates General of the Netherlands in Mumbai and Bangalore, at the Netherlands Business Support Offices in Ahmedabad and Hyderabad and the Dutch Honorary Consuls in Lucknow, Kolkata and Chennai. We call it the Dutch Trade Network in India and, as you can see, we are present in eight metropoles in India.

***

H.E. Venu Rajamony, Indian Ambassador to the Netherlands, Indian Embassy

"The Netherlands is an economic powerhouse and the 4th largest investor in terms of FDI inflows to India. Between 2015-18 infact, around US $8 billion worth of investments have gone into India from the Netherlands"

- **How has been your experience so far in The Netherlands?**

  My experience in the Netherlands has been outstanding. The Netherlands is a beautiful country with friendly people and an international outlook. Indian Prime Minister Narendra Modi's visit in 2017 marked a high point in Indo-Dutch relations and the upcoming visit of Prime Minister Rutte to India in May 2018 will provide significant new momentum to our long standing relations. What is truly amazing to me is the tremendous potential there is for a win-win partnership between India and the Netherlands in many fields. While the Indian economy is currently exhibiting growth rates of 7.5%, the Dutch economy has also been showing steady growth, increasing by 3.1% in 2017 compared to 2016. The Netherlands is an economic powerhouse and the 4th largest investor in terms of FDI inflows to India. Between 2015-18 infact, around US $8 billion worth of investments have gone into India from the Netherlands. It is the second largest exporter in the world of agro products, is the leading healthcare sector in Europe as well as a world leader on all matters relating to water. There is much that our two countries, people and businesses can do together.

- **What are the key sectors that you would recommend to Indian companies looking at the Netherlands based on your experience?**

  There are number of sectors in which Indian companies can benefit from collaboration with Dutch companies. Agriculture and food processing is a priority sector in India where the Netherlands has significant strengths in terms of technology, entrepreneurship and the ability to invest abroad. India is in the process of implementing massive programmes to build infrastructure. We have set ourselves an ambitious goal to generating 175 Giga Watts of energy from solar and other forms of renewable energy by 2022. We have launched programmes such as Stand-up India; Start-up India; Digital India; Skill India; Make-in-India; Clean India Mission;

Mission for Rejuvenation and Urban Transformation; Housing for All etc where there are many complementarities with the skills and capability of Dutch companies. There is also great potential for collaboration in areas like Smart Cities and Cyber Security. I would strongly recommend that Indian companies visit the Netherlands and explore various opportunities that can lead to mutual benefit.

- **How do you see the evolvement of India-Netherlands business relationship (past, present and future)?**

Business relations between India and the Netherlands have evolved from what used to be a one way street to a two-way street. There are today as many Indian companies operating in the Netherlands as there are Dutch companies in India. Companies from the Netherlands such as Philips, Shell and Unilever have been in India for several decades and are household names. Similarly, Indian companies are rapidly growing in the Netherlands and there are reports from across the country of more and more Indian families and students moving to this country. Some of the biggest groups from India like Tata Steel and TCS have a long standing presence in this country and contribute significantly to providing job and bolstering the economic strength of the Netherlands.

I see our relationship becoming bigger and bigger as well as even more diverse in the coming years. Despite the close economic and political relationship between the two countries, there is still considerable lack of knowledge regarding each other amongst the people of the two countries. This information gap needs to be bridged. I encourage companies of both sides to take an interest in each other and visit each other, to explore opportunities both in each other's countries as well as jointly in third countries. I give particular emphasis to small and medium enterprise of the Netherlands in this regard. It is important that small, medium, family owned companies of the Netherlands take interest in India proactively take advantage of the opportunities that are available in India. Indian companies see the Netherlands as a country with a welcoming environment. Indian companies are already using the Netherlands as a gateway to Europe and a hub for their investments across Europe.

- **What can be done further to promote The Netherlands as a location for Indian companies? Any recommendation or suggestion you would like to give for further boosting of India-Netherlands relationship? Given the situation of Brexit, what would the Netherlands do to make it attractive for Indian companies as a gateway to Europe?**

My recommendation for further strengthening India-Netherlands relations is that the two countries maintain a steady level of high level as well as business contacts. We must strengthen our mutual investment and trade and at the same time also promote exchanges in the field of science and technology. There is also need for greater people to people contacts including exchange of tourists, cultural figures and groups as well as students and faculty.

- **Any word of caution/challenges that Indian companies should be aware of while investing into the Netherlands?**

Indian companies should study the laws and system of the Netherlands well before commencing operations in this country. They should make sure that they do not in any manner violate any of these laws.

***

Stans Kleijnen, Executive Director, NFIA India
"Most international companies really love being based in the Netherlands because of its international atmosphere and business climate. They appreciate the efficiency, transparency and "gezelligheid" (coziness) of the people"

- **What is the role and function of NFIA India?**

  NFIA India is the focal point for Indian companies looking at expanding to the Netherlands. Based in Mumbai, Delhi and Bangalore we are in the same timezone as our customers and can be in touch quickly to assist them with any questions they have regarding their expansion plans. Our services include providing information about the tax system, the business climate, visas and making connections with service providers such as tax lawyers, accountants, realtors and recruiters.

- **Why is the Netherlands considered a gateway to Europe?**

  The Netherlands is strategically located in the center of Europe from where you can reach 170 million customers within 300 miles. The Netherlands has excellent connectivity to the rest of Europe by air, train, waterways and roads and is often used as a hub. Additionally, the local workforce is highly fluent in English and many other common European languages.

- **Having lived in India for quite some time, what may Dutch and Indian companies want to consider when doing business with each other to create a stronger and more sustainable business relationship?**

  I moved to India in July 2015 and before that worked for NFIA in San Francisco for 6 years. I have found the professionalism of the companies in India and the US to be quite similar. The best guarantee for an effective business relationship is to communicate clearly and frequently so that expectations are managed well. The Dutch are very direct (often perceived as blunt) and Indian nationals often tend to being less specific and more focused on building relationships. If both nationalities meet halfway, success will be very likely.

- **How would you describe your experience of international companies using the Netherlands as a European headquarters location?**

  Most international companies really love being based in the Netherlands because of its international atmosphere and business climate. They appreciate the efficiency, transparency and "gezelligheid" (coziness) of the people. The fact that most people speak English also helps them to feel at home quickly. Companies typically see their business pick up substantially after setting up in the Netherlands.

- **Are there any subsidies/grants for assistance from the Dutch government to promote certain sectors which could be of use for Indian companies?**

  Most incentives are embedded in the tax system, varying from the Innovation Box for R&D related activities to grants for energy efficient buildings and the 30% ruling for individual taxes. For specific details please contact NFIA to get personalized information.

- **Any word of caution/challenges that Indian companies should be aware of while investing into the Netherlands?**

  The laws and processes in the Netherlands are well defined and transparent and the system works best when information is shared proactively. This is especially important for opening a bank account as the European-wide rules and regulations are tightened in recent years because of more scrutiny in financial markets.

***

Jolanda van der Aart, Sr. Manager Foreign Investments – Head of India Desk, Amsterdam in Business

"The Amsterdam Area act as a magnet for European & Global Head-offices, IT & Tech companies, Financial services, media, food, gaming , aerospace, logistics, life-sciences and pharmaceutical companies, and start-ups"

- **What makes Amsterdam a unique and favored destination for Indian companies to set up their offices/headquarters here?**

Amsterdam is connected to the rest of Europe and the world – not only by an extensive transport network and the world's largest internet hub, but also by the city's collaborative approach to doing business.

Amsterdam's spirit of commerce and excellent quality of life make it a magnet for talent, startups and international headquarters for companies from across the globe.

Main reasons for Indian business for selecting Amsterdam:

• Great business ecosystem

• Well connected by land, water and air

• Digital and social connectivity

• Access to talented workforce

• High quality of life

• Fantastic cultural life

Amsterdam offers a wide network of internationally orientated service providers who offer companies a competitive edge. We connect people and businesses in key sectors to our ecosystem and invite them to grow with us. We love to connect on a personal level but also excel as a logistic hub, on- and offline.

Amsterdam also is the place to be for startups and has always been a natural testbed for innovations. Throughout the city, fresh and disruptive ideas are encouraged, nurtured and then scaled into real international businesses. Nurturing this growth, the city is home to an impressive ecosystem of accelerators, incubators and high-ranking knowledge institutions.

When compared to other major international cities, we are especially competitive in regards to costs for office space, housing, labor, utilities, transportation and effective corporate tax rates.

Many international employees in Amsterdam can take advantage of significant personal tax allowances. The 30% reimbursement ruling (better known as the 30% ruling) is a tax advantage for highly skilled migrants moving to the Netherlands for a specific employment role. When the necessary conditions are met, the employer can grant a tax-free allowance equivalent to 30% of the gross salary subject to Dutch payroll tax.

Amsterdam ranks below many other European cities when it comes to cost of living.

Amsterdam also boasts a modern, productive, flexible and internationally oriented workforce. Education levels are high: the Dutch education system is widely renowned and Amsterdam's higher education offering ranks among the world's best.

In addition, the majority of Amsterdam's residents speak English well and are often fluent in one or two languages on top of that.

There are over 180 nationalities in the city, with thousands of students, geeks, marketers, engineers and founders biking their way around the city, and numerous tech and startup academies where people educate and re-educate themselves.

Thanks to its great work-life balance, cultural agenda and more, Amsterdam is a wonderful place to live and work in.

Amsterdam attracts plenty of internationals to work in industries such as IT, creative, finance, life sciences and fashion. The renowned work-life balance, lively cultural scene and laid-back lifestyle are key benefits of working and living in Amsterdam, making it a popular place to relocate to.

People from all over the world are attracted to the livability and quality of life found throughout the region, resulting in a strong international workforce; in addition, Amsterdam is one of the most multicultural cities in the world. The city is home to 180 different nationalities, and 90% of its residents speak English, making it easy to do European and worldwide business.

- **What help and benefits can Amsterdam provide Indian companies?**
  We are the official partner of the Netherlands Foreign Investment Agency (NFIA) for the Amsterdam Area and offer customized solutions by providing Indian companies who plan to set up in the Amsterdam Area with relevant information. As we are part of the Dutch government services are **free, confidential and without obligation.**

  We provide:

  Market Intelligence: providing specific data on markets, industries and sectors.

  Investment climate: providing information about the Dutch tax climate, incentives, legal & regulatory framework and labor market.

  Fact-finding visits: tailor-made fact-finding programmes to get informed about the fiscal climate, the market, availability of talent, business climate and quality of service providers, and to visit office locations.

  Legal & tax advice: organizing free introduction meetings with internationally-oriented business service suppliers to elaborate on legal and fiscal structures that meet your current and long-term needs.

  Talent: tapping into the labor market via introduction to recruiters and/or networks and communities of professionals.

  Business & partner networks: introductions to strategic partners, business networks/associations, knowledge institutions, tax authorities, governmental agencies and when through our network, potential clients.

  Relocation support: assistance in search and selection of temporary, flexible and permanent office space including site visit tours.

  Support for international staff: apartment search for expats(short stay/long stay), introductions to international schools, expat clubs and referrals to doctors.

- **What sectors/clusters are best represented in Amsterdam? [EMA]**
  We are regarded an excellent "Gateway to Europe" for Indian companies: whether you are an established business that's looking to grow or a global corporate expanding to Amsterdam, a new startup doing things differently, connectivity counts.

  The Amsterdam Metropolitan Area offers full access to the European market: the award-winning Amsterdam Airport Schiphol is centrally located and flies to more than 300 destinations. High-speed rail services connect from Amsterdam to Brussels, Paris, London and Berlin. Many companies from India already set up their European Headquarters here.

Amsterdam's connectivity is not limited to **logistics.** The Amsterdam Metropolitan Area is a thriving **tech hub**, too, and home to the largest data transport hub in the world, the Amsterdam Internet Exchange (AMS-IX). The region also has the highest broadband penetration in Europe.

Amsterdam is renowned as a top-level international financial services and business centre.

It houses all major Dutch financial institutions as well as branches and subsidiaries of more than fifty prominent European and international banks. Combined with a strong legal and services sector this creates an energetic global business environment Amsterdam.

Recently, the European Medicin Agency (EMA) has announced that they will relocate from London to Amsterdam in 2019 which is expected to attract **Pharma, Lifesciences & Consultancy companies.**

As a result, the Amsterdam Area act as a magnet for European & Global Head-offices, IT & Tech companies, Financial services , media, food, gaming , aerospace , logistics, life-sciences and pharmaceutical companies, and start-ups.

- **How has Amsterdam benefitted over the past years with Indian companies doing business here in the city?**
  The interaction with Indian companies goes both ways. For Amsterdam and The Netherlands as a whole, the Indian expats bring knowledge and expertise which is relevant for our economy (such as knowledge on block-chain, machine learning, and artificial intelligence). Furthermore, every expat accounts for 2-3 additional jobs, as expats require housing, go to international schools and have good spending power.

  The fact that the Amsterdam Area hosts over 3200 International companies- most of them European head-offices, represent a great opportunity for Indian companies as they tap into these potential clients for business deals. In addition, with Amsterdam Schiphol Airport close by – The Netherlands has become the hub for mainland Europe from which it is easy to enter into the European market.

Early adopters such as Tata Consultancy Services, Infosys, Sun Pharma, Wipro\Technologies have established offices or factories in the region. As a result, the Netherlands as a whole is home to the second-largest Indian community in mainland Europe, comprised of approximately 215,000 people (including Hindustan community with roots on India) . The highest numbers of highly skilled migrants to take advantage of IN Amsterdam's services are from India and there is much in the region to make the Indian community feel at home.

- **What is the latest trend of Indian companies investment into Netherlands especially in light of Brexit?**

  Amsterdam has a long history as a successful business hub and leading centre of trade. Over 3.200 international companies have established offices in the Amsterdam Metropolitan Area. In 2017, 143 new international companies chose to open an office in our region.

  After the referendum, we saw an increase in requests for information from international companies and we have set up a team dedicated to businesses from the UK. However, what Amsterdam is doing to attract international businesses – worldwide has not changed much since Brexit.

  Our proposition on what Amsterdam has to offer foreign, amongst them Indian companies remained the same: excellent physical and digital connectivity, and a highly skilled workforce are among the advantages for businesses. Amsterdam is seen as a Gateway to Europe.

  For some businesses, being located in the European Union / mainland Europe is important and we think that the Amsterdam area is a viable alternative. An example is the European Medicines Agency (EMA) that will relocate to Amsterdam when it leaves London in 2019 with 900 staff members.

  From India we see a lot of interest from IT, Tech, Pharma companies & interest to set up European Head-offices.

- **Does Amsterdam has the necessary infrastructure to handle efflux of Indian migrants and companies?**

  Amsterdam has set up a dedicated India Desk back in 2006 when the "BRICS" countries came into focus.

Connectivity is very important: 2 years ago, the prominent carrier Jet Airways has set up their European Headquarters at Amsterdam Schiphol Airport. They have since entered into a joint venture agreement with KLM and offer direct flights to Delhi, Mumbai and Bengaluru. In addition, KLM offers direct flights to Delhi and Mumbai. The number of direct flights between India and The Netherlands increased from 7 to 31 per week over the past year.

For newcomers from India, we have the IN Amsterdam center (an Expatcenter set up 9 years ago). The Indian Expat is the largest group we welcome at our expanded brand new International Newcomers Centre at the World Trade Centre Amsterdam.

It is a one-stop shop for acquiring a work permit and registration with the City governments. At the same time we provide information on all aspects of settling in- such as setting up a bank account, international schools, housing, health-services, obtaining drivers-licence .

Besides this, there is much in the region to make the Indian community feel at home.

For instance, there are many international schools that offer a bilingual education, the Hospitals have set up a dedicated India Desk for health advice, and there are various dedicated non-profit organisations, such as the Netherlands India Chamber of Commerce & Trade, Netherlands-India Association, Bridging the Gap who support Indians when settling in.

Amsterdam inbusiness organises the India Cricket day and supports the Annual Diwali Festival in Amstelveen. In addition, both ASSOCHAM and Indian Institute of Chartered Accountants in India have set up their European Chapters in Amsterdam. So, there is a vibrant Indo-Dutch ecosystem in the Amsterdam Area.

***

Lars de Vries, Sr. Manager Foreign Investments – India, Brabant Development Agency

"Out of the 200 Indian companies, our small region hosts almost 30 companies from India including the large corporates like Wipro, Infosys BPO, Cognizant, Tata Steel Tubes, RF Solutions, Banco Products and many other small and innovative firms like Forthcode, Intech DMLS. Combining strength on both sides in our new digital realm of 3D printing, IoT, Data Analytics and AI"

- **What makes Brabant a unique and favoured destination for Indian companies to set up their offices/headquarters here?**

We believe in cooperation and our region has a strong connection with India. With the city of Eindhoven being the hometown of Philips, also present in India for the past 100 years, many IT companies have found their business relations with the front-runners in co-creation. Also, global companies from the region like NXP and TomTom have a large and committed history with India which has led to an intensive traffic of knowledge and people between the two countries.

But not only the corporates are there, also the lively start-up scene and the SME's are especially important for us. The company of Eindhoven Medical Robotics Technologies is a great example of this. It provides advanced knowledge and technologies, assisting surgeons to do the impossible with their RoBoSculpt, with the ability to navigate autonomously in high precision bone surgery. A very promising technology start-up, incubated at the Technical University of Eindhoven, which intends to ramp up to a 1000+ people team, utilizing the collaborative R&D network between the Netherlands and India, using the scale of the market that India offers.

From the Indian side we see a similar movement. Out of the 200 Indian companies, our small region hosts almost 30 companies from India including the large corporates like Wipro, Infosys BPO, Cognizant, Tata Steel Tubes, RF Solutions, Banco Products and many other small and innovative firms like Forthcode, Intech DMLS. Combining strength on both sides in our new digital realm of 3D printing, IoT, Data Analytics and AI.

Besides the business aspect, there is also a thriving Indian community and we believe that, after Amsterdam, Eindhoven hosts the largest and fastest growing Indian Expat

Community of the Netherlands with around 3000 Indian people. Resulting in the fact that some 30% of the population on our International School is Indian. The Indian community is organized in at least 8 different groups related to major states in India and the Indo-Dutch Association Eindhoven. All organizing cultural events throughout the year, including Diwali, Ugadi and of course Cricket matches and Bollywood nights.

And when it comes to business, Brabant has a lot to offer. Our extensive ecosystems in high tech, logistics, chemicals, life sciences, aerospace and agrifood take collaboration possibilities to a new dimension. Moreover, global industry leaders are interwoven with world renowned knowledge institutes and government.

You can find easy access to 170 million Europeans within 300 km of Brabant's central location. No more than 90 minutes away from major cities like Amsterdam and Rotterdam in the Netherlands, but due to its proximity to the German and Belgium borders you can reach cites like Dusseldorf, Antwerp and Brussels in the same time. World-class airports, top-ranked seaports and high-speed road, rail, water and broadband networks are on your doorstep. This combined with an abundance of real estate means Brabant is the perfect starting point for distribution

In Brabant, we have talented people that love to engage and share with others. They welcome collaboration and use it daily to learn, innovate, find solutions to global issues as well as to socialize. Our highly educated people pride themselves on being open-minded, eager to share, welcoming and helpful. Knowledge sharing is applauded and effortless collaboration and networking with high performing industry experts is a way of life here.

- **What sectors/clusters are best represented in Brabant?**

High Tech and IT

If it's the complete HTSM value chain you need - from R&D, manufacturing to assembly and distribution – you're in the right place. With our 100-year heritage in mechanical engineering, Brabant is a melting pot for High Tech Systems and Materials (HTSM) meaning an abundance of high tech expertise is guaranteed. A fifth of all Dutch HTSM-related jobs and 25% of production are based here. With half of the country's R&D spend originating from Brabant, it's no surprise that more patents are filed from here than from anywhere else in the Netherlands.

Known as the smartest city in the Netherlands, Eindhoven - with its High Tech Campus - is ranked third worldwide in the Forbes Foreign Direct Investment Index for best innovation hubs. The High Tech Campus unites technology and 11,000 highly qualified people from globally renowned R&D institutes and knowledge centers. This unique "Brainport" district, offers an unbeatable environment for open innovation.

Also of interest for India is the Automotive sector with a:

- Strong reputation for busses, trucks and special vehicles
- High concentration of automotive component companies
- Many automotive related companies in chemistry (materials), electronics & communication technology
- Access to Europe's major automotive markets: Germany, France and UK
- 88% of business are exports
- High Tech Automotive Campus in Helmond
- Special focus on green mobility and smart mobility

Logistics

Brabant ticks all your boxes when it comes to your logistics critical success factors – ideal location, available real-estate and sophisticated infrastructure. But on top of all that, we have a special magic that out-does all other locations: our people! This makes your logistics in Brabant cost effective and as stress free as possible.

"Tilburg enables us to optimize our logistics and gives us excellent access to continental Europe where we deliver as many cars as in North America."

Elon Musk – Tesla

But, of course the region ticks all the other logistic checklist boxes as well:

- Location

  You are centrally situated between Rotterdam and Antwerp – two of the world's biggest seaports, and close to Amsterdam, Eindhoven, Brussels and Dusseldorf Airports, so ideal for your international imports and exports. Your direct neighbors are Belgium and Germany, with France and the UK only a stone's throw away.

- Real Estate

  Available and affordable space is at your fingertips.

- Infrastructure

  Your transportation becomes multi-modal by road, air, rail and water and all major shipping companies have hubs here. You reduce your telecommunications costs here as they are the second lowest in the world.

- Reliability

  Dependable, effective and trustworthy, your logistics consistently run smoothly thanks to the pro-business attitude of customs authorities as well as a favorable tax environment with VAT deferment possibilities.

- Speed

  Time wasting here is taboo! Whether you are setting up, enhancing or ensuring the smooth running of your daily logistics, up and running is the order of the day!

- Collaboration

  Innovation through collaboration is deeply ingrained in our DNA so it's no surprise that the Dutch Institute for Advanced Logistics (TKI DINALOG) is based here. You have access to its work on continuous improvement through knowledge sharing, experience and results.

- **What help and benefits can Brabant provide Indian companies?**

At BOM Foreign Investments we believe that investing in Brabant, the Netherlands is the solution for foreign companies looking to optimally invest in Europe; and we strive to make it happen. We facilitate all aspects of foreign direct investment in Brabant by offering personalized guidance through the site selection process and providing relevant and up-to-date information and links to our extensive network; services we continue to provide to companies with an established presence in Brabant. BOM Foreign Investments is part of the Brabant Development Agency (BOM), established in 1983 and funded by the Dutch government and the province of Brabant.

BOM is an official partner of the Netherlands Foreign Investment Agency (NFIA), and we communicate on a daily bases with their team India. All geared to optimize our support for the Indian companies.

In short, we help companies to:

SAVE TIME
Direct introduction to organizations, networks and institutes that are relevant for your company, such as government, knowledge institutes, industry and commercial service providers.

SAVE MONEY
Information about subsidies, incentives, possible tax benefits and funding opportunities that may be applicable to your company.

STRENGTHEN YOUR INTER-COMPANY POSITION
Information to build a business case for your head office to expand your activities, such as benchmarking the Netherlands and Brabant. Connections to local networks and suppliers to benefit from your location.

SUPPORT WITH TALENT ISSUES
New ways to find talent, answers to labor law and visa questions as well as cross cultural advice and links to universities and international schools.

HELP WITH LEGISLATION
Advice in matters with regards to rules, regulations and permits because of our direct links with relevant authorities.

AND OUR SUPPORT IS FREE OF CHARGE AND CONFIDENTIAL.

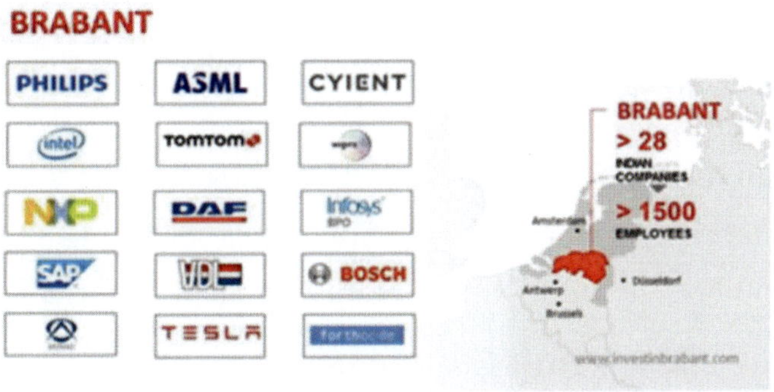

Chris van Voorden, Director-Foreign Investments, InnovationQuarter

"Our objective is to stimulate economic growth in our region. One of our tasks is Foreign Investments; promoting the region abroad in order to attract and support foreign companies to set up their business in West Holland"

- **What is the role and function of the InnovationQuarter?**

  InnovationQuarter is the regional economic development agency for West Holland. Our objective is to stimulate economic growth in our region. One of our tasks is Foreign Investments; promoting the region abroad in order to attract and support foreign companies to set up their business in West Holland. Furthermore, we also invest in innovative companies and set up business consortia around new, promising innovations.

- **What key sectors are represented by the InnovationQuarter and how can Indian companies (including start-ups) benefit from it?**

  We work for and with all strong sectors in our region. The main focus sectors are: Safety & (cyber) Security, Life Sciences & Health, Hightech & Smart Industry, Clean Technology, Aerospace, Horticulture, and Maritime & Offshore. Indian companies are very welcome to come here and participate in these sectors. Benefits are access to (European) market, access to talent (with three world renowned universities in our region: Erasmus University Rotterdam, Delft University of Technology and Leiden University) and access to capital (through our three investment funds or other venture capital funds, active in our region).

- **What are the challenges for Indian companies when starting their business in the Netherlands?**

  In general, setting up a business in the Netherlands is fairly easy. Challenges are the same for all (foreign) companies, setting up a new business: finding the first customers and finding the right talent to build up the local organization.

- **The Dutch trade mission 2018 is scheduled to take place in May 2018 and has a specific focus on the agri and food sector, water management and life sciences.**

What do you expect from this mission and do you have any suggestions as to how the results may be maximized by both the Netherlands and India?

This is going to be an exciting mission, covering some key sectors in which we are also active in. Let's not forget the cyber security focus as well, especially interesting for us as we have already various contacts in that field; mainly in Hyderabad and Bangalore, together with The Hague Security Delta. The results can be maximized by looking for joint opportunities in an open and transparent way; this should not be an issue, as I have had very positive previous experiences in working with the Indian business world.

XII. Team: ASSOCHAM & NFIA

ASSOCHAM Netherlands Team	NFIA India Team
Dr. Vikas Chaturvedi Chairman, ASSOCHAM Europe (Netherlands) info@assochamnetheralnds.org	**Stans Kleijnen** Executive Director stans@nfia-india.com
Prachee van Brandenburg Secretary General p.vanbrandenburg@assochamnetherlands.org	**Swati Sudhakaran** Senior Project Manager swati@nfia-india.com
Sandra Singh Head, Indian Investments in the Netherlands s.singh@assochamnetherlands.org	**Pritam Prashar** Senior Project Manager pritam@nfia-india.com
Peyoush Datta Head, Dutch Investments in India p.datta@assochamnetherlands.org	**Balaji Venkatraman** Senior Project Manager balaji@nfia-india.com

References

Annual Report 2016-17
http://commerce.gov.in/writereaddata/uploadedfile/MOC_636281140249481285_annual_report_16_17_eng.pdf

Trade policy review report by the secretariat the European Union, May 2017
https://www.wto.org/english/tratop_e/tpr_e/s357_e.pdf

Trade policy review report by the European Union, May 2017
https://www.wto.org/english/tratop_e/tpr_e/g357_e.pdf

https://www.dnb.nl/en/news/news-and-archive/persberichten-2017/dnb359927.jsp

Understanding logistics in The Netherlands
http://www.cbre.eu/portal/pls/portal/res_rep.show_report?report_id=261

Doing Business in Netherlands,2017
https://www.pwc.nl/nl/assets/documents/pwc-doing-business-in-the-netherlands-2017.pdf

Investment in the Netherlands, KPMG,2016
https://assets.kpmg.com/content/dam/kpmg/pdf/2016/07/Investment-in-the-Netherlands-2016.pdf

Netherlands Foreign Investment
https://en.portal.santandertrade.com/establish-overseas/netherlands/foreign-investment

Invest Holland
https://investinholland.com/economic-overview/at-a-glance/

EY's attractiveness survey Netherlands Attractiveness Survey 2016 From investment to long-lasting confidence
http://www.ey.com/Publication/vwLUAssets/EY-netherlands-attractiveness-survey-2016/$FILE/EY-netherlands-attractiveness-survey-2016.pdf

The Global Innovation Index 2017 Innovation Feeding the World
https://www.globalinnovationindex.org/gii-2017-report

The Global Competitiveness Report 2017–2018, World Economic Forum
http://www3.weforum.org/docs/GCR2017-2018/05FullReport/TheGlobalCompetitivenessReport2017%E2%80%932018.pdf

Logistics
https://www.hollandalumni.nl/files/documents/career/factsheets-key-sectors/factsheet-logistics

Royal Schiphol Group Annual Report,2016
https://www.unglobalcompact.org/system/attachments/cop_2017/366191/original/Schiphol_Group_Annual_Report_2016.pdf?1489046519

Schiphol placed into perspective A study on the growth of the Dutch hub airport in relation to the growth of competing European airports G.D. Koeveringe (386340) - Rotterdam, July 31, 2017 Erasmus School of Economics - Erasmus University Rotterdam Bachelor of Science (BSc) in Economie en
file:///C:/Users/home/Downloads/Koeveringe-GD-386340-BA-thesis.pdf

Study of the economic market power on the relevant market(s) for aviation and aviation-related services on the Amsterdam Airport Schiphol Final version
http://userpage.fu-berlin.de/jmueller/gapprojekt/downloads/gap_papers/finalreport.pdf

Schiphol Group Annual Report,2015
file:///C:/Users/home/Downloads/Schiphol_Annual_Report_2015.pdf

Importance of Logistics Performance Turkey
https://www.itf-oecd.org/sites/default/files/docs/15cpb_logistics-turkey.pdf

U.S. Department of State on Netherlands
https://www.state.gov/documents/organization/228194.pdf

Source: Information Technology The Netherlands
https://investinholland.com/nfia_media/2015/04/NFIA_InformationTechnology_Brochure2016.FINAL_.WW_.pdf

Region Profile of European Union (EU) Doing Business 2018 Indicators
http://www.doingbusiness.org/reports/~/media/WBG/DoingBusiness/Documents/Profiles/Region al/DB2018/EU.pdf

Doing Business 2018, South Asia
http://www.doingbusiness.org/reports/~/media/WBG/DoingBusiness/Documents/Profiles/Region al/DB2018/SA.pdf

Ministry of Infrastructure &Environment, THE NETHERLANDS Home to leading maritime companies
file:///C:/Documents%20and%20Settings/arvind.kumar/My%20Documents/Downloads/14806_001_MIN_Infrastructuur%2526Milieu_Vlaggenbrochure_Update_2016_12_HR_Di...%20(2).pdf

Connecting the world through global shipping networks Jan Hoffmann1*, Gordon Wilmsmeier2 and Y.H. Venus Lun, Hoffmann et al. Journal of Shipping and Trade (2017) 2:2 DOI 10.1186/s41072-017-0020-z
https://www.springeropen.com/track/pdf/10.1186/s41072-017-0020-z?site=jshippingandtrade.springeropen.com

PPT on LSCI
https://www.unece.org/fileadmin/DAM/trans/events/docs/logistics_dec09_s2_unctad.pdf

PPT on Holland Logistics
http://www.ndl.nl/wp-content/uploads/2017/05/Marketing-propostie-High-Tech-final.pdf

Economics of Connectivity
https://www.asef.org/images/docs/3.%20Economics%20of%20Connectivity.pdf

https://www.export.gov/article?id=Netherlands-Market-Overview

World Economic Outlook, October,2017, IMF
file:///C:/Documents%20and%20Settings/arvind.kumar/My%20Documents/Downloads/text%20(6).pdf

Embassy of India, The Hague, the Netherlands
http://www.indianembassy.nl/eoi.php?id=Trade

Facts & Figures, Port of Rotterdam
https://www.portofrotterdam.com/sites/default/files/facts-and-figures-port-of-rotterdam-2016.pdf

Invest in Holland Network
https://investinholland.com/invest-in-holland-network/

The Europe 2020 Competitiveness Report,2014 edition
http://www3.weforum.org/docs/WEF_Europe2020_CompetitivenessReport_2014.pdf

Reserve Bank of India (RBI), Annual Report, 2016-17
https://www.rbi.org.in/Scripts/AnnualReportPublications.aspx?year=2017

export.gov
https://www.export.gov/article?id=Netherlands-Labeling-Marking-Requirements

Netherlands - 7-State Owned Enterprises
https://www.export.gov/article?id=Netherlands-State-Owned-Enterprises

Netherlands - Import Requirements and Documentation
https://www.export.gov/article?id=Netherlands-Import-Requirements-and-Documentation

Netherlands Standards for Trade
https://www.export.gov/article?id=Netherlands-Trade-Standards

List of companies with Dutch government shareholding
https://www.rijksoverheid.nl/onderwerpen/staatsdeelnemingen/vraag-en-antwoord/in-welke-ondernemingen-heeft-de-overheid-aandelen

CE marking
http://europa.eu/youreurope/business/product/ce-mark/index_en.htm

Dutch Banking
https://www.ebf.eu/about-us/the-netherlands/

U.S. Department of State on Dutch Economy
https://www.state.gov/documents/organization/228194.pdf

The Netherland-A trading nation
https://www.hollandtradeandinvest.com/feature-stories/the-netherlands-a-trading-nation

First published in India in 2018

Published By:

Invincible Publishers

G-120, Sushant Lok III, Sector 57, Gurgaon-122002

Registered Address: Opposite Kasturba Ashram, Radaur, Haryana - 135133

Printed at Thomson Press (India) LTD